GLORIOUS
PERVERSITY

MORE WILDSIDE CLASSICS

Dacobra, or The White Priests of Ahriman, by Harris Burland
The Nabob, by Alphonse Daudet
Out of the Wreck, by Captain A. E. Dingle
The Elm-Tree on the Mall, by Anatole France
The Lance of Kanana, by Harry W. French
Amazon Nights, by Arthur O. Friel
Caught in the Net, by Emile Gaboriau
The Gentle Grafter, by O. Henry
Raffles, by E. W. Hornung
Gates of Empire, by Robert E. Howard
Tom Brown's School Days, by Thomas Hughes
The Opium Ship, by H. Bedford Jones
The Miracles of Antichrist, by Selma Lagerlof
Arsène Lupin, by Maurice LeBlanc
A Phantom Lover, by Vernon Lee
The Iron Heel, by Jack London
The Witness for the Defence, by A.E.W. Mason
The Spider Strain and Other Tales, by Johnston McCulley
Tales of Thubway Tham, by Johnston McCulley
The Prince of Graustark, by George McCutcheon
Bull-Dog Drummond, by Cyril McNeile
The Moon Pool, by A. Merritt
The Red House Mystery, by A. A. Milne
Blix, by Frank Norris
Wings over Tomorrow, by Philip Francis Nowlan
The Devil's Paw, by E. Phillips Oppenheim
Satan's Daughter and Other Tales, by E. Hoffmann Price
The Insidious Dr. Fu Manchu, by Sax Rohmer
Mauprat, by George Sand
The Slayer and Other Tales, by H. de Vere Stacpoole
Penrod (Gordon Grant Illustrated Edition), by Booth Tarkington
The Gilded Age, by Mark Twain
The Blockade Runners, by Jules Verne
The Gadfly, by E.L. Voynich

Please see www.wildsidepress.com for a complete list!

GORIOUS PERVERSTY

The Decline and Fall of Literary Decadence

by
BRIAN STABLEFORD

WILDSIDE PRESS

GLORIOUS PERVERSITY

This edition published in 2006 by Wildside Press, LLC.
www.wildsidepress.com

CONTENTS

Acknowledgments 4

PART ONE: THE ORIGINS OF THE DECADENT WORLDVIEW

1. Civilization Grown Old: The Idea of Decadence 6
2. *Le Spleen de Paris*: Charles Baudelaire and the Decadent
   Style 15
3. The Cult of Artificiality: The Development of Decadent
   Consciousness 26
4. *A Rebours*: Joris-Karl Huysmans and the Decadent Manifesto ...41
5. Extraordinary Sensations: Disease, Disorder and Decadence 54

PART TWO: CASE STUDIES FROM THE DECADENT MOVEMENT

6. *Masques*: Jean Lorrain and the Decadent Quest 68
7. Angels of Perversity: Rémy de Gourmont's Retreat from the
   World 84
8. *The Torture Garden*: Octave Mirbeau and the Politics of
   Decadence 97
9. The Decay of Lying: Oscar Wilde and the English Decadent
   Movement 108
10. *Fin de Siècle*: The Decadent Heritage............................. 124

Notes 138
Selected Bibliography 140
Index.. 144

ACKNOWLEDGMENTS

Parts of Chapters I, III, V, VIII, IX, and X are derived from the introduction to *The Dedalus Book of Decadence (Moral Ruins)* (1990). Parts of Chapters IV, V, IX, and X are derived from the introduction to *The Second Dedalus Book of Decadence (The Black Feast)* (1992). Chapter VI is derived from the introduction and afterword to Jean Lorrain's *Monsieur de Phocas* (1994), Chapter VII from the introduction to Rémy de Gourmont's *The Angels of Perversity* (1992), and Chapter VIII from the introduction to Octave Mirbeau's *Torture Garden* (1990). All the volumes in question were published by Dedalus; some of the relevant items were signed "Francis Amery."

PART ONE

THE ORIGINS OF THE DECADENT WORLDVIEW

I.

CIVILIZATION GROWN OLD:

THE IDEA OF DECADENCE

The English word "decadence," and its French counterpart *décadence*, derive from the Latin *cadere*, to fall. The kind of fall indicated thereby, however, is a special one, as is signified by the verbs to which the nouns are parent: the obsolete *décair* in Old French and "decay" in English. To decay is to rot, to fall away from a state of health into a gradual ruination. We sometimes think of death as the starting-point of decay, but it is not; nor is it the end. Within the human body the processes of aging begin to take effect before we are born. Decay is our lifelong companion: a shadow within, whose empire slowly spreads to take command of our flesh; even while we are growing we are also "falling," gradually but inexorably, towards dissolution. Death is merely an intermediate punctuation mark in the convoluted sentence of decay.

In 1734 Charles-Louis le Secondat, Baron de La Brède et de Montesquieu, published his *Considérations sur les causes de la grandeur des Romains et de leur décadence*. The essay was marred by a certain disregard for the full extent and exact implication of the factual evidence, but it was nevertheless an important work, in that it sought to discover some kind of theoretical basis for historical explanation. For Montesquieu, the slow disintegration of the Roman Empire was not to be seen as a series of unhappy accidents, but as the inevitable unfolding of a pattern governed by a quasi-scientific law: a law whose governance still applied to the modern world.

Whatever its faults as proto-social science, Montesquieu's work was rightly acclaimed as a bold adventure of the intellect, and the case which he put forward was eventually enshrined in common parlance as an element of modern folklore. Rome, it was henceforth accepted, had fallen because all empires must fall, and the map of that fall—which was also to serve as an explanation—was to be found in its *décadence*: in the simultaneous rotting of its cultural life and its military might.

The chief anti-hero of this fable was the Emperor Nero, who allowed the political fabric of the empire to become corrupt while he entertained his court with extended examples of his (imagined) literary genius. The decadence of his mind was exemplified by the legend which claimed that he played upon his fiddle while Rome burned around him; the decadence of his morals was readily revealed by the fact that his mimicry of the affectations of the Greeks extended as far as marriage to a castrated male slave. Other emperors with equally nasty inclinations, like Caligula and Heliogabalus, were given minor roles in the melodrama.

The first translator who rendered Montesquieu's *Considérations* into English did not retain the word "decadence" in its title, choosing to render *décadence* as "declension," but the term had its effect nevertheless. The British were by far the most successful of modern Imperialists, and were much given to drawing parallels between their own enterprise and the Augustan era of Rome. It is not at all surprising that it was an Englishman, Edward Gibbon, who undertook to repair the factual inadequacies of Montesquieu's work and to offer a minute and scrupulous analysis of *The Decline and Fall of the Roman Empire*.

The first volume of Gibbon's work, published in 1776, quickly achieved notoriety because of the uncharitable treatment afforded to the birth and early evolution of Christianity by its concluding chapters; he saw the conversion of the crumbling empire to the new religion simply as one more stage in its decline. For Gibbon, Rome had briefly achieved an altogether admirable ideal, and his account of the empire's fall is redolent with a special sense of tragedy; for all its cynicism his was essentially a Jeremiad: a Book of Lamentations. Thus was the myth of Rome's decadence amplified and set in stone.

Montesquieu, in claiming that there was an underlying logic to the fate of Rome, implied that some such pattern could and would be repeated in other empires. Any empire, in this view, was likely to carry within its body politic the seeds of its own destruction. Any secure, rich, and comfortable aristocracy would inevitably tend to a slow enervation by addiction to luxury, until the time finally arrived when the barbarians lurking beyond the borders could no longer be kept at bay.

* * * * * * *

Montesquieu's attempt to discover a nexus of causes in the historical record was entirely in tune with what later writers, looking back on the ambitions and achievements of the eighteenth century, have called the Age of Enlightenment. In Montesquieu's wake came a host of philosophers intent on finding explanations of the patterns of history which would complement the understanding of the physical world developed by men like Laplace and Newton in the previous century.

Montesquieu's own subsequent contribution to the debate, *De l'esprit des lois* (1748) was disappointing, concentrating primarily on the influences of climate and geography upon the development of civilization, but it was followed in 1750 by two far more dramatic—and dramatically opposed—adventures in historical analysis.

Anne-Robert Jacques Turgot never wrote the discourse on "universal history" which he sketched out in two lectures which he gave at the Sorbonne in 1750, but he nevertheless succeeded in giving a considerable boost to the notion which was to dominate French social thought during the second half of the century: the idea of Progress. Turgot conceived "universal history" as the story of the entire human race, which was, he contended, advancing by slow degrees—albeit neither uniformly nor steadily—towards a state of social perfection. Although history exhibited phases of calm and disturbance, Turgot claimed, these were merely the incremental steps of progress, which was driven not by reason but by the insistent passions of men. In this view, dark ages such as the one which followed the fall of Rome were to be regarded as pauses paving the way for the emergence of a better society than the one which had been put away.

This idea proved enormously influential; it was taken up and worked out in more detail by Turgot's friend and biographer the Marquis de Condorcet, and by the men who compiled the great *Encyclopedia* between 1751 and 1765. It was popularized by Louis-Sébastien Mercier in *L'An 2440* (1770), the first Utopian novel to place its ideal society in the future—in Paris!—rather than on some remote island. It was one of the motive forces of the revolution of 1789, helping to justify the violent overthrow of the *ancien régime*, whose own alleged decadence came to be widely seen as a stumbling block to the great cause of Universal Progress.

It was also in 1750, however, that Jean-Jacques Rousseau suddenly emerged from obscurity to win a prize offered by the Academy of Dijon for the best essay on the subject of whether the arts and science had conferred benefits on mankind. It is always an advantage in competitions of that kind to take the unfashionable side, in the interests of seeming original, and to go to extremes, in the interests of seeming daring. Rousseau contended that science and the arts were, in fact, the worst of all the enemies of morality by virtue of creating and increasing wants, thus paving the way for many evils; the "noble savage" was in his view the very model of the ideal and moral man. He may have taken such a line initially for purely strategic reasons, but having been awarded the prize he elected to stick fast to it, and having become famous, he spent the rest of his life elaborating the thesis.

In 1754 Rousseau entered a similar discourse on the origins of inequality for a similar prize, but he had lost the advantage of startlement and he did not win; even so, the published essay set the seal on his reputation. It held that men were innately good, but that their nature was warped by the institutions of civilization so that they became bad. He lamented the introduction into human affairs of agriculture and metallurgy, contending that grain and iron were the root causes of modern unhappiness. For Rousseau, in short, everything that Turgot calculated as progress was really to be reckoned degeneration. He continued to elaborate this thesis in his novel *La Nouvelle Héloïse* (1760), his treatise on education *Émile* (1762), and his treatise on politics *Du Contrat social* (1762), establishing a field of dissent which drew opponents of the theory of progress like a magnet, and armed them with iconoclastic arguments with which to express their scepticism.

* * * * * * *

The clearing away of the French *ancien régime* added further confusion to debates about nature, civilization, history, and progress. Within two years the revolution had spawned the Terror, and there is a certain terrible irony in the fact that the Marquis de Condorcet had to write his *Esquisse d'un tableau historique du progrès de l'esprit humain* (1795) while he was in hiding from Robespierre. Shortly after finishing it he was caught, and the exact circumstances of his subsequent death in prison remain unclear.

There was, of course, another Marquis who became ironically caught up in the revolution, whose writings were—even more so than Rousseau's—the very model of outrageous opposition to conventional wisdom. The Marquis de Sade was released from long imprisonment by the Revolution and was appointed as a judge by the revolutionary tribunal, in which capacity he was a sore disappointment to his masters. He explained his reluctance to issue death sentences by contending that, although committing crimes for pleasure was both understandable and excusable, it was against his principles to commit murder in the name of justice.

In a series of calculatedly scandalous works Sade took up arms against conventional ideas of morality by extolling the excellence of everything that they condemned, most especially that which was considered indefensible. He punctuated his epic tales of torture, buggery, and coprophilia with extensive homilies on the follies and fallacies of institutionalized morality. The banning of the *La Philosophie dans le boudoir* (1795) and *La Nouvelle Justine* (1797), which added *L'Histoire de Juliette* to the third version of *Justine, ou les malheurs de vertu* ensured—as such bans generally do—that it remained in urgent demand for the following century and a half, an obligatory study for anyone and everyone interested in any form of dissent. *Les 120 journées de Sodome*, written in the Bastille in 1785, shortly before the first version of *Justine*, remained long unpublished and unread, but not unrumored.

The philosophy of Sade is, in a sense, the logical conclusion of the oppositional line taken by Rousseau. Rousseau had attacked civilization by extolling the goodness of Nature; Sade ruled that goodness itself was an unnecessary and undesirable social construct, that Nature—the only source to which men can and ought to look for guidance—licenses any and all acts. Furthermore, Sade argued, there is a particular pleasure to be obtained from the violation of laws and commandments, and no sound reason why those who have the power to do so should decline the opportunity to indulge themselves in its sharp delights.

Sade did, in fact, raise and luridly dramatize an important moral question: given that God does not exist, what force can moral commandments possibly have? The fact that those who opposed him refused to answer the question, trying with all their might to pretend that it could not even be asked, only lent weight to the suspicion that no adequate answer was available. The suppression of Sade's works created the appearance that their message was a secret too monstrous to be revealed, but it was never any secret that the message in question argued the essential falsity of all the pretensions and affectations of civilization and its mores.

Sade was removed from the revolutionary stage when he was committed to the asylum at Charenton for allegedly writing a pamphlet attacking Napoléon and Joséphine (of which crime he appears to have been innocent). He eventually died there in 1814, the year in which Napoléon's fabulous adventure in European Imperialism came to its first conclusion with the emperor's banishment to Elba. For ten years Napoléon had seemed to many observers to be the modern Julius Caesar, and Paris the new Rome—a possibility that was briefly renewed in 1815 but quickly foundered at Waterloo.

The monarchy whose corruption had been a favorite topic of the Revolutionists was more-or-less restored after Napoléon's final exile, but it was a weak and sickly thing by comparison with its predecessor, and for the next century France seesawed between royalism and republicanism. The year of revolutions, 1848, brought another Napoléon, who served initially as an elected president, but launched a *coup d'état* in 1851 and became emperor the following year. He was eventually deposed by invading Prussian forces at Sedan in 1870; in the following year Paris fell under the control of the Commune, which subjected the city to a further dose of post-Revolutionary Terror.

While all this was going on it became easy enough for Frenchmen to believe that the nation, and all it had represented in the long-gone days of the "sun king" Louis XIV, was on a slippery slope headed for oblivion. Such was the temper of the times, though, that it was possible to contemplate this prospect with attitudes which filled an extensive spectrum between outright delight to bleak despair, and included many curious alloys of the two.

* * * * * *

Rousseau's works had made particular appeal to followers of the cult of *sensibilité*, which applauded expression of the emotions and was suspicious of the products of the intellect. This cult, which existed before he offered it an argumentative basis, was considerably strengthened by his input, and was thus enabled to mount more strenuous opposition to the conventional wisdom of the day.

Philosophy had long worked with images of divided human nature, whose "higher" element was the power of reason, and its "lower" element the unruly passions. Almost without exception philosophers had followed Plato in approving of the former while deploring the latter, which were frequently regarded as a subversive threat to peace of mind. The philosophers of progress inevitably saw progress in terms of an increasing empire of reason, and they looked forward to an eventual annihilation of what Descartes had stigmatized as primitive "animal spirits." The advocates of *sensibilité* did not succeed in raising much opposition to this dominant view among the champions of the Enlightenment, but they did have a considerable influence on the aesthetic theories that became the inspiration of the Romantic Movement, which swept through Europe at the end of the century.

The aesthetic theories of the Romantics were scornful of utilitarianism; they did not like that which was rational and functional. Their notion of beauty extolled all that was wild, not merely in nature but also in matters of artifice. They disliked architectural styles which submitted to the dictates of mechanical efficiency, preferring instead the calculated extravagance of the highly-ornamented "Gothic" style which had flourished between the twelfth and fifteenth centuries. They also disliked formal gardens, preferring a mannered simulation of wilderness, into which ready-made ruins were sometimes inserted. Their revolt against the Enlightenment also let them to a fascinated interest, if not to actual belief, in the occult and the supernatural.

The fad for neo-Gothic architecture also gave birth in England to the Gothic novel. Horace Walpole, the progenitor of the neo-Gothic mansion Strawberry Hill, pioneered the new fashion in literature with *The Castle of Otranto* (1765), in which a haunted castle provides a stage for the working-out of an ancestral curse, which reaches its climax with the simultaneous destruction of the edifice and its corrupt inheritor. The villain of the piece, Manfred, set in place a much-imitated stereotype: a tormented soul hovering on the brink of insanity, prey to incestuous lusts and megalomaniac ambitions which threaten to overwhelm and devastate his innocent victims. William Beckford, inhabitant of a more extreme adventure in neo-Gothic architecture, Fonthill Abbey, offered as a literary counterpart the phantasmagorical Oriental tale *Vathek* (1786), whose eponymous anti-hero is perversely impatient to follow the descending path of his illicit desires all the way to eventual damnation in the Halls of Eblis.

Although the Gothic novel shared the disrepute which all novels then had, and failed to win the redemption from that disrepute that the realistic novel eventually attained, its concerns and affectations soon spread to more reputable art forms. Wordsworth and Coleridge provided the English Romantic movement with a manifesto of sorts in the preface which they added to the second edition of *Lyrical Ballads* at the dawn of the nineteenth century, while August Schlegel was compiling a similar manifesto for the German movement.

While the values of the Enlightenment stressed the objectivity of reason, the Romantic rebellion upheld the subjectivity of individual experience. While the Enlightenment philosophers aimed to cultivate an impersonal, organized, and disciplined knowledge of scientific laws, the Romantics cultivated a personal, intuitive, and inchoate sense of the infinite and the transcendental. The Romantics were not, however, opposed to the idea of progress, and were mostly committed to what they considered to be progressive causes; the second generation of British romantics, led by Byron and Shelley, were certainly not enmired by nostalgia for a lost past. Many Romantics considered the civilization which had spawned them to be "decadent," and many lamented the ugly utilitarian fruit of the Industrial Revolution which was gathering pace around them, but they conceived of themselves as rebels in search of a better way forward. By means of their reverence for Nature and their carefully-nurtured "sensibility," they hoped to found a new Utopia instead of a Dark Age; they did not believe that modern men were doomed to repeat the worst errors of their Roman forebears.

* * * * * * *

Amid their many other achievements the English Romantics laid the foundations of "Literary Satanism," which may be said to have spring from a remark made in 1793 by William Blake to the effect that Milton, in writing *Paradise Lost*, had been "of the devil's party without knowing it." What he meant by this was that although Milton's declared purpose in writing *Paradise Lost* had been "to justify the ways of God to man," the poet had instead made Satan's rebellion against divine authority both comprehensible and admirable.

Shelley amplified Blake's judgment in his *Defence of Poetry* (1821). He wrote:

> Milton's poem contains within itself a philo-
> sophical refutation of that system, of which, by a
> strange and natural antithesis, it has been a chief pop-
> ular support. Nothing can exceed the energy and
> magnificence of the character of Satan as expressed in

Paradise Lost. Milton's Devil as a moral being is as far superior to his God as one who perseveres in some purpose, which he has conceived to be excellent, in spite of adversity and torture, as to one who in the cold security of undoubted triumph inflicts the most horrible revenge upon his enemy....with the alleged design of exasperating him to new torments.

Blake and Shelley were, of course, prepared to practise what they preached. Blake's "prophetic books" developed his own alternative mythology in which Orc, the son of Los and Enitharmon, bursts the bonds which enchain him to become a heroic rebel against Urizen, the tyrannical deviser of moral codes. Shelley's *Prometheus Unbound* (1820) offered a similar account of revolution and redemption, in which the tyrant Jupiter is vanquished and a new era of liberty and harmony ensues. Both writers found it convenient, for diplomatic reasons among others, to substitute other figures for the Satan of the Christian Mythos, but they nevertheless set a pattern for the issuing of strident challenges to the moral authority of the Church. Their proposal that the image forged by the Church to embody its notion of evil was neither hateful nor despicable, but actually heroic, paved the way for a redrafting of the map of good and evil which was far subtler than that of Rousseau and somewhat more sophisticated than the brutally frank iconoclasm of Sade.

It is not particularly surprising that it was English writers who set this particular train of thought in motion, given that England had by now accumulated a long history of religious dissent; France, being a Catholic country, had only a muted history of argumentative dissent. On the other hand, those dissenters to whom France did play host were prone to go to further extremes; the profusion of modest protestant heresies held few attractions for them, and when they lapsed from the faith or took up arms against it they had no truck with half-measures. Nor is it surprising, therefore, that the first notable work of explicit literary Satanism came not from England but from France, or that the work in question should come from the pen of a man who reacted against all the vast confusion of conflicting intellectual and aesthetic positions that had been mapped out in the previous century.

The writer in question was Charles Baudelaire, who published "Les Litanies de Satan" in *Les Fleurs du mal* (1857), a collection of poetry which managed the phenomenally difficult task of setting itself up in opposition to everything. It refused Enlightenment and Romanticism alike. It refused to agree with Rousseau that Nature was good and it refused to agree with Sade that Nature had no morality at all. It was scornful of all belief in progress but was equally scornful of any retreat towards primitivism. It embraced a new view of the world and it devised a new style, by means of which its novel worldview might be appropriately displayed. While its author was alive this worldview and its attendant style had no name, but as soon as he was dead it acquired one, by courtesy of an enthusiastic introduction added to the third edition of the collection.

Théophile Gautier, who provided that introduction, was by then the leading figure of the French Romantic Movement and its chief chronicler. There was no one better placed to judge exactly where Baudelaire fitted into the kaleidoscopic confusion of theses and antitheses which had provided the context of his work, and no one better equipped to pin a label on him. The label Gautier chose was "Decadent." In choosing it he undoubtedly had Montesquieu in mind, but he nevertheless took great pains to say exactly what this new application of the word signified. His remarks provided the first rough sketch of the manifesto which, a generation later, became the inspiration of the French Decadent Movement.

II.

LE SPLEEN DE PARIS:

CHARLES BAUDELAIRE
AND THE DECADENT STYLE

According to Théophile Gautier,

> the style of the decadence [is] no other thing than Art
> arrived at that point of extreme maturity that deter-
> mines civilizations which have grown old; ingenious,
> complicated, clever, full of delicate hints and refine-
> ments, gathering all the delicacies of speech, borrow-
> ing from technical vocabularies, taking color from ev-
> ery palette, tones from all musical instruments, con-
> tours vague and fleeting, listening to translate subtle
> confidences, confessions of depraved passions, and
> the odd hallucinations of a fixed idea turning to mad-
> ness.

Such a style is, Gautier states, "summoned to express all and to
venture to the very extremes." Baudelaire's work recalls to his mind

> language already veined with the greenness of decom-
> position, savoring of the Lower Roman Empire and
> the complicated refinements of the Byzantine School,
> the last form of Greek Art fallen into deliquescence;
> but such is the necessary and fatal idiom of peoples
> and civilizations where an artificial life has replaced a
> natural one and developed in a man who does not
> know his own needs.

Gautier goes on to say of Decadent style that

> Contrary to the classical style, it admits of back-
> grounds where the specters of superstition, the hag-
> gard phantoms of dreams, the terrors of night, re-

morse which leaps out and falls back noiselessly, obscure fantasies that astonish the day, and all that the
soul in its deepest depths and innermost caverns con-
ceals of darkness, deformity, and horror, move together confusedly.[1]

The first great flourish of this distinctive style was, of course,
unkindly received. The pump of scandal had been primed by eighteen
poems which had previously been published in *Le Revue des deux mondes* in 1855, and the publication of *Les Fleurs du mal* two years later
was the signal for legal action to be taken. The Court imposed a heavy
fine on the author and ruled that six of the hundred-and-one poems
("Les Bijoux," "Le Léthé," "A celle qui est trop gaie," "Lesbos,"
"Femmes damnées," and "Les Métamorphoses du vampire") were to be
suppressed as obscene.

The fine was eventually reduced in 1858. Its effects were further ameliorated by the fact that Baudelaire received in that year a grant
from the Minister of Public Education for the translations of Edgar Allan Poe which he had begun in 1848 (the year before Poe's death).
Even so, the fact that it was hanging over him may well have compounded the deterioration of his health, which was continual after 1857.
Baudelaire continued to work as best he could, but he was in dire financial straits by 1861, and his fortunes became irreparable when his publisher fled to Brussels in 1862 to avoid bankruptcy, ruining plans for a
third edition of *Les Fleurs du mal*; the third edition was not to appear
until 1868, the year after Baudelaire's death at the age of forty-six.

The cruelly paradoxical forces which shaped his character and
equipped his worldview are easy enough to identify in Baudelaire's biography. His father, born in 1759, and his mother, born in 1793, were
the products of very different eras of French history. From his father—
who had been tutor to an aristocratic family and had absorbed enough
of their elegance and refinement to side with them against the Revolutionists—Baudelaire inherited luxurious tastes and the expectation of a
considerable legacy of money. Unfortunately, his mother quickly remarried following the elder Baudelaire's demise in 1827 (when Baudelaire was six years old), and her new husband, Captain Jacques Aupick,
was not at all the same kind of man as his predecessor.

Although it had been partly spent in anticipation of its arrival,
Baudelaire's inheritance was ultimately withheld from him by his stepfather and half-brother, whose standards of respectability he had begun
to disappoint while he was a clever but troublesome schoolboy. He was
expelled from school for lack of discipline, although he went on to
complete his bachelor's degree in 1839. When he subsequently declined to prepare himself for any other career than writing, he was un-
ceremoniously packed off on a long sea voyage in the hope of
"removing him from evil influences," but sea travel did not agree with

him, and his fascination with the Orient was not adequate to arm him against its effects. He spent some weeks in Mauritius, but turned back before reaching his intended destination, India.

Baudelaire's return to France in 1842 was construed by his relatives as further evidence of his irresponsibility. The debts which he quickly ran up and his infatuation with the mulatto actress Jeanne Duval added to their anxieties. The Aupicks then took measures to ensure that he spent the rest of his life in unnecessary poverty, the periodic remittances which they doled out to him via a legally-appointed guardian never being adequate to redeem his debts. His subsequent attempts to make a living with his pen were always resentfully half-hearted.

* * * * * * *

Within the space of this spoiled life, Baudelaire found no adequate cause for joy or satisfaction. His relationships with women provided little solace and much heartache; the love-poems which he wrote are redolent with pain and frustration, whether they refer to his sexual liaison with Duval—his "Black Venus"—or to his doomed attempts to pursue a love affair with the uncaringly capricious actress Marie Daubrun in 1847. The poems inspired by the Salon-keeper Madame Sabatier in 1852 are so odd and ambivalent as hardly to warrant consideration as love-poems at all, although they include one of those condemned as obscene ("A celle qui est trop gaie"). Once he split with Duval, he seems to have led an almost ascetic existence, although the state of his health probably precluded any other.

Nor could Baudelaire find any satisfactory release from his misery in his experiments with drugs. Gustave Flaubert complained of his essay on hashish and opium, *Les Paradis artificiels* (1860), that what had begun as a pioneering exercise in natural science had been overtaken by a preoccupation with the spirit of evil supposedly incarnate in these substances. Gautier recalled that Baudelaire had been markedly reluctant to involve himself in the "experiments" undertaken by "le Club de Hachischins"—which included Gérard de Nerval as well as Gautier—on the grounds that a flight from necessary sorrow must be inherently Satanic.

Given his willingness to address litanies to Satan, this reluctance and its ostensible grounds might seem eccentric. Baudelaire declared on his own account that he wrote *Les Paradis artificiels* to demonstrate that seekers after artificial paradises inevitably create private hells. This seems to have been his invariable experience, and must have been even more marked in his pursuit of erotic fulfillment than in his half-hearted quest for psychotropic transcendence; it was probably from his Black Venus that he caught syphilis.

Baudelaire's miseries were further compounded by the fact that his work was not well-received by his contemporaries—at least, not openly. He decided to offer himself as a candidate for the Académie Française in 1861, but was advised to withdraw by Charles-Augustin Sainte-Beuve, whom he had idolized, and whose novel *Volupté* (1834) was one of the main precursors of his own literary endeavor. In 1844 Baudelaire had written an "epistle" in verse proclaiming that he had imported the story into his heart, absorbing all its "miasmas" and "perfumes," and that he had become a practitioner of the same "cruel art" as its protagonist Amaury, but Sainte-Beuve always refused to return the compliment, off-handedly condemning Baudelaire's work as "folly."

Another who was openly scathing about Baudelaire's work, although he might have been expected to be sympathetic, was Jules-Amédée Barbey d'Aurevilly, whose own cynical dandyism was saved from being thoroughly Decadent only by his devout Catholicism. D'Aurevilly remarked that the only two possibilities open to the man whose soul was revealed in *Les Fleurs du mal* were conversion to Catholicism and suicide. (Baudelaire had already wounded himself attempting suicide in 1845, and appears always to have regarded himself as an "incorrigible"—though permanently lapsed—Catholic.)

Théophile Gautier, who evidently understood him far better, unfortunately hoarded his own praise until after Baudelaire's death. The only poet who seems to have given Baudelaire a useful measure of moral support while he was alive was the only one who condescended to give an oration at his funeral: his long-time friend Théodore de Banville, the most outspokenly enthusiastic supporter of Gautier's doctrine of "art for art's sake." We can now see the significance of the fact that two admiring essays on Baudelaire's work were published in 1866 by Stéphane Mallarmé (who was then twenty-three) and Paul Verlaine (who was then twenty-one), but Baudelaire had no way of knowing what these young men would become. He could have had no notion of the reputation that he would rapidly acquire after his death, and no idea that he would one day become the father-figure of an entire literary movement.

The unfortunate and bitterly frustrating life which Baudelaire led was the force against which his work reacted, but the precise form of his reaction was determined by factors of another kind. Many of the ideas which he took up had descended through the intellectual debates mapped out in the previous chapter, filtered through generations of literary activity. Just as the Decadent worldview had its philosophical precursors, so the Decadent style had its literary precursors.

Most of Baudelaire's sources of inspiration are obvious. Gautier's analysis of the value of Baudelaire refers to elements which can also be found in a few of his own works, and might have stood out more strikingly had he not been so very prolific. Baudelaire acknowledged his own debt to Sainte-Beuve and also credited the example of Aloysius Bertrand's *Gaspard de la nuit* (1842) as an important factor in his decision to experiment with prose-poetry. These were the primary precursors of the Decadent style in Baudelaire's own country, and the only other French name which needs to be added to the list is that of Auguste Barbier. There is, however, one other writer whose influence was of enormous importance, perhaps greater than any or all of these four. Inevitably, Baudelaire took a great deal of inspiration from the work which occupied him for much of his adult life, whose bulk outweighed his own slender produce: his translations of the works of Edgar Allan Poe.

* * * * * * *

The French members of this group were all closely associated with the Romantic Movement, although all of them drifted away from it. The whims of fashionability are such that literary movements hardly have time to be born before someone is reacting against them and someone else is trying to transcend them; so it was with French Romanticism.

The triumphant arrival of Romanticism in Paris was trumpeted by the *claque* which turned out at the first night of Victor Hugo's *Hernani* in 1830. Prominent among these enthusiasts was the nineteen-year-old Théophile Gautier, who had made certain that he would not pass unnoticed by wearing a shocking pink waistcoat. Gautier followed up this *coup de théâtre* by becoming the most fervent and extravagant of the French Romantics and the author of the (inevitably) unfinished *Histoire de romantisme*, but his wildest experiments in Romanticism eventually tested the optimism of the Romantic outlook to destruction.

Gautier never tired of writing wildly Romantic fantasies in which idealistic young men, frustrated by the crassness of the modern world, escape into liaisons with fabulous supernatural women: the eponymous courtesans in "Omphale" (1834) and "Arria Marcella" (1852), and the Egyptian Princess Hermonthis in "Le Pied de momie" (1840). Even when the attentions of these *femmes fatales* promise to be literally fatal, as in the case of the hectic affair between a novice priest and a vampire in "La Morte amoureuse" (1836; usually translated as "Clarimonde"), the author's opinion seems to be that the price is worth paying. In none of these stories, however, does the power of the Romantic impulse succeed in forging a firm and permanent link between the aspiring hero and his supernatural inamorata. The loss of supernatural ecstasy is regarded as a tragedy of matchless proportions, but it is also regarded as an inevitable outcome of reckless ambition.

Gautier himself seems to have lived in uneasy suspension between the allure of ideal love and the second-rate consolations of real-life sex; he nursed a determinedly high-minded passion for the dancer Carlotta Grisi while making a mistress of her sister Ernesta. In his art and his life alike he revealed the hopeless folly of the Romantic idealization of love and its promise of eupsychian fulfillment. Only one of

19

Gautier's fantasies—*Spirite* (1865), which he wrote specifically for Carlotta Grisi—concludes with a satisfactory consummation, but it is (necessarily) postponed until the afterlife.

Gautier's importance as a precursor of the Decadent style is secured by three works: *Mademoiselle de Maupin* (1834), *Fortunio* (1837), and "Une Nuit de Cléopâtre" (1838). All three provide portraits of unusual characters whose highly idiosyncratic worldviews and exotic lifestyles are treated with envious sympathy.

Mademoiselle de Maupin is a long and teasing essay in studied eroticism in which the hero's search for ideal passion is confused by his confrontation with the eponymous heroine in male disguise; his arguments in justification of the presumed homoerotic attraction are then applied to the heroine's seduction, while in male guise, of a page who also turns out to be a girl in male clothing. The flirtatiousness of the novel, augmented by its careful prefatory essay affirming the doctrine of art for art's sake, saved it from demolition by the charges of indecency which were inevitably brought against it, and allowed it to prepare the ground for the more intense celebrations of homoeroticism to be found in the works of Verlaine and Lorrain, and for the paeans of praise for Lesbianism which were to be sung by Baudelaire and Pierre Louÿs.

The eponymous hero of *Fortunio* comes to Paris from the East, establishing for himself an exotic microcosm where tropical lushness is simulated by cunning artifice so that he might feel "at home." In this novella we meet for the first time the Decadent personality languishing in its unnatural habitat, more-or-less content to drift on the tides of ennui while half-heartedly buoyed up by the elaborate contrivances of artifice. Like Gautier's fabulous *femmes fatales*, *Fortunio* is essentially a dream which cannot persist, but he is offered to the reader as a powerfully attractive dream.

Gautier's Cleopatra, who similarly enjoys an existence made almost unbearable by comfort and luxury, is more persuasive than the entirely fictitious and slightly fatuous Fortunio as an image of the perfect object of erotic desire. She seeks relief from the terrible burden of her ennui and obtains momentary distraction in the arms of a lover, who then gladly consents to be put to death when the return of Mark Antony is signalled. The fact of his execution is incorporated into the queen's aesthetic experience, making it complete, and winning the unparalleled tribute of a single covert tear. It was this story and *Mademoiselle de Maupin*, more than any others, whose echoes Gautier heard resounding in the style and manner of Baudelaire's work.

Auguste Barbier's scathing attacks on political corruption and other assorted social evils had influenced Victor Hugo's work, but Barbier had too little faith in the rewards of idealism to become a wholehearted Romantic, and he always remained on the fringes of the movement. Barbier's three most important collections of poetry, *Iambes*

(1831), *Il pianto* (1833), and *Lazare* (1837), condemned life in modern Paris and lamented the sad decline of Italy from its glorious past, but found no hope in Romantic rebellion.

Barbier's work helped to popularize two terms which were later to become central to the Decadent vocabulary: ennui and spleen. Unlike Gautier, however, Barbier was highly critical of the enervation and debauchery arising from fashionable ennui and he had not the slightest sympathy with its capricious and spiteful extension into spleen. According to him, men of a splenetic disposition inevitably went completely to the bad, under the influence of drugs, drink, and sexual perversion. This attitude disqualified him from becoming a true proto-Decadent, but his satirical method left open the possibility that the sarcastic tone might be removed or ignored, thus converting demolition into celebration. Barbier did, however, lay the groundwork for the so-called Parnassian poets, who elected to disapprove of the emotional heat of Romanticism, preferring to adopt a more detached and studious approach to its typical imaginative products. Although the echoes of his work—somewhat deformed and transmogrified—do resound in *Les Fleurs du mal*, they are more clearly echoed in the work of Théodore de Banville and his followers.

Sainte-Beuve's association with Victor Hugo was close enough at one time to allow him to fall hopelessly in love with the elder poet's wife, but his subsequent adventures in literary criticism led him to desert the Romantic fold and to denigrate his former idol. Sainte-Beuve abandoned the aesthetic theories of Romanticism for a species of critical eclecticism which regarded a poet's work as a map of his personality. His own literary criticism thus became a form of psychological portraiture.

Although it was founded on the principle that a writer's work should always be approached sympathetically, this manner of procedure inevitably led to a situation where the critic found himself condemning the work of men whose morals he did not much like, and this was why he condemned Baudelaire's work as folly. Before he embarked upon this path, however, Sainte-Beuve had produced a curious and condemnatory self-analytical work of his own in *Volupté*.

Volupté became an important model of the way in which contradictory impulses might combine to produce a Decadent sensibility. Amaury, the disastrously apathetic hero of the novel, is caught between his ideal passion for the unattainable Madame de Couaën and his lustful adventures with the whores of Paris. Unable to sustain the philosophical tensions in his life, he eventually renounces his uncomfortable scepticism, recommits himself to the Catholic faith, and emigrates. It was, of course, Amaury's early experiments in living rather than his final reinvestment in traditional values that attracted Baudelaire to the book.

It was Sainte-Beuve who arranged for posthumous publication of Aloysius Bertrand's *Gaspard de la nuit*, Bertrand having become his closest friend after the split with Hugo. Bertrand's *Gaspard de la nuit* is more important as an experiment in form than for its contents, but they do reflect the Romantic interest in the "Gothic." They are very whimsical, and have none of the anguished seriousness of Baudelaire's most heartfelt prose-poems, but they are possessed of a certain charming morbidity and have a hallucinatory quality which goes beyond their manifest interest in dreams. In borrowing the form that Bertrand had originated, Baudelaire must have wondered what the poet might have produced had he not died so young (he was thirty-four).

* * * * * * *

All of these writers had some effect on Baudelaire, but none of them had anything like the effect of Edgar Allan Poe. Barbier, Gautier, and Sainte-Beuve were Baudelaire's neighbors, and yet they remained very distant; Poe was no longer alive and the product of a nation whose shores were thousands of miles away, and yet Baudelaire lived in close intimacy with him for most of his adult life.

Baudelaire did not simply read Poe, he rewrote Poe into the French language—and he rewrote almost all of Poe, including items which hardly anyone bothered to read in the original English. If there was any other human being with whom Baudelaire felt a profound intellectual kinship it was Poe; the fact that Poe is still revered as a great writer in France, while he is remembered with faint embarrassment in America, is largely due to the efficacy of Baudelaire's translations.

Like Baudelaire, Poe had had a stepfather who, though relatively wealthy, refused to support his literary career. Like Baudelaire, Poe had felt that his mother had remarried beneath her, and that he was nobler than his stepfather by reason of blood and temperament alike. Like Baudelaire, Poe had lived perennially beyond his means, seeking but not finding solace in escapist dreams, whose produce he made into an art form. It is hardly surprising that Baudelaire thought himself a like mind, or that he took the lessons which he learned from Poe's poetry and short stories very much to heart.

Baudelaire's fascination with Poe's *Tales of the Grotesque and Arabesque* went beyond mere matters of method. He understood the way in which Poe's doomed aristocrats reflected, albeit perversely, Poe's image of himself. He also understood the way in which Poe became increasingly enamored of his own eccentricities, to the point that he became far more interested in magnifying than correcting them. He understood, therefore, the curious amalgam of comedy and seriousness which went in to such fantasies as the description of C. Auguste Dupin's lifestyle which introduces "The Murders in the Rue Morgue."

Thanks to his benefactor, who has gone to "the expense of renting, and furnishing in a style which suited the rather fantastic gloom of our common temper, a time-eaten and grotesque mansion," the relentlessly eccentric Dupin is able to live a secluded life, admitting no visitors and going out only by night. "It was a freak of fancy in my friend," the narrator observes,

> to be enamored of the night for her own sake; and into this bizarrerie, as into all his others, I quietly fell; giving myself up to his wild whims with a perfect abandon. The sable divinity would not herself dwell with us always; but we could counterfeit her presence. At first dawn of the morning we closed all the massy shutters of our old building; lighted a couple of tapers which, strongly perfumed, threw out only the ghastliest and feeblest of rays. By the aid of these we then busied our souls in dreams—reading, writing or conversing until warned by the clock of the advent of the true Darkness.[2]

This passage combines the most significant aspects of Decadent literary style with what was to become the Decadent philosophy of life: a calculated inversion of conventional values which rejoices in retreatism, escapism, and Gothic self-indulgence. This was probably more significant than anything he read in the French renegade Romantics to Baudelaire's fascination with flowers of evil and the aesthetics of perversity. When Baudelaire progressed from the poetry of *Les Fleurs du mal* to the prose-poems which he intended to collect as *Le Spleen de Paris* (but which had to be published posthumously in Volume IV of his *Oeuvres complètes* as *Petits Poèmes en prose*), he must have had Poe's "Shadow—a Parable" (1835), "Silence—a Fable" (1838), and "The Masque of the Red Death" (1842) in mind as well as *Gaspard de la nuit*.

* * * * * * *

Although it is the poems collected in *Les Fleurs du mal* that continue to define Baudelaire's literary reputation, it is the sequence of his works in prose that offers the clearest and most coherent account of the evolution of his attitude to the world.

Baudelaire's earliest work of prose fiction—which he sometimes listed as the earliest of all his works—was the novella *La Fanfarlo*, written in 1843-44 and published in 1847. It is the work of a young man blithely refusing to take himself too seriously, mocking the pretensions of Romantic poets. Its protagonist is Samuel Cramer, a poet whose natural endowment of ability is devoured by idleness, by virtue of his being "a gentleman by birth and something of a rakehell by way of amusement." He is "a fantastic and maladapted character, who displays his poetry more brilliantly in his person than in his works."

23

He seems to the narrator a kind of "modern and hermaphrodite god," but a god of impuissance whose powerlessness is "so vast as to be epic in its proportions." After years of piety he has become a passionate atheist, and although he can adapt himself to become any writer he has ever read, he remains "profoundly original."

The adventure in which this mercurial hero becomes involved is appropriately absurd. He is captivated by Madame de Cosmelly, but she only takes an interest in him in order to commission him to break up a romance which has developed between her husband and a dancer named Fanfarlo. He succeeds in attracting the attention of the dancer by attacking her in print, explaining himself by confessing his ardent love for her, and wins her heart. When Cramer casually lets it drop that he was hired to seduce her from her former lover, however, she rejects him—at which point the passion which he has so far only simulated becomes real, and renders him so utterly wretched that he turns to socialism and plans a political career.

All these jokes were to turn sour under the burden of Baudelaire's subsequent misfortunes. He never lost the ability to contemplate his own failings with a certain wry scorn, but the stresses of his existence turned his good humor into blackly comic desperation as he realized what it actually meant to be a "god of impuissance." This evolution can be tracked through a quartet of prose-poems which begin as lyrical hymns to escapism and end as sarcastic acknowledgments of the inescapability of fate.

"L'Invitation au voyage" (written 1857; published 1862) is the most hopeful and self-indulgent of the group, conjuring up a vision of the legendary earthly paradise of Cockayne which is offered to the poet's lover with all due enthusiasm, but then begins to fade. "Dreams, always dreams!" the poet laments. "The more adventurous and sensitive the soul is, the further dreams transport it from the possible. Every man carries within himself an appropriate measure of natural opium, incessantly secreted and replenished...and yet, between birth and death, how many hours can we count to the credit of positive pleasure, or of actions planned and carried out?"[3] In this case, the fading of the dream is followed by a defiant renewal; it is the lover herself, the poet concludes, who contains and conjures up this vision of an ideal existence.

There is no sign of a human lover in "La Chambre double" (1862), in which the poet imagines himself in a wonderful room where "the soul bathes in idleness, amid the aromas of regret and desire," where "the furniture too seems to be dreaming" and "the fabrics speak a language of silence." This vision is inhabited instead by an invisible Goddess whose "eyes....burn bright in the twilight; subtle and terrifying mirrors of the soul, whose fearful malice I know so well." No sooner has the poet achieved the estrangement he seeks, declaring that "Time is banished; it is Eternity which rules this place: an Eternity of delights!" than he is recalled to reality by a knocking on the door and

24

he sees his room as it actually is: a "tawdry place of infinite tedium" where "the rankness of desolation lies upon everything," and the only object which can bring a smile to his place is a vial of laudanum. Time's empire is restored and the burden of mundanity reimposed: "Sweat, slave! Live, and be damned!"[4]

The bitter irony of "La Chambre double" is further echoed in "Les Tentations, ou Éros, Plutus et la Gloire" (1863), in which the dreaming poet is visited by three demonic tempters. The first offers to appoint him "an overlord of souls," whereby he might become "a greater master of living clay than any sculptor could ever be of his own material," and enjoy "the pleasure, perpetually renewed, of emerging from thyself to forget thyself in others, and of drawing souls to merge with thine own." The second offers him power: "that which will obtain everything, which hath infinite value, which replaceth anything whatsoever."[5] He rejects these offers out of hand, but when the third offers him worldly fame, he concedes that it is something worth having, only turning her away when he remembers the company he will have to keep. Reflecting on his experience, however, the awakened poet can only wish, plaintively, that the tempters might one day return to repeat their offers while he is in a more sensible frame of mind.

Rueful irony gives way to frank desperation in "Anywhere Out of the World" (1867), whose title—given in English in the original—is derived from Thomas Hood's morbid poem about the suicide of an outcast young woman, "The Bridge of Sighs" (1843). The piece begins by comparing life to a hospital in which every invalid is obsessed with the desire to occupy a different bed; the poet interrogates his soul as to where, exactly, he might go to find comfort, but the soul remains deaf to all his practical suggestions, only replying when the impatient interlocutor resorts to satirical exaggeration. The soul's reply is that anywhere will do, so long as it is outside the world.

Such was the trajectory followed by Baudelaire's attitude to the world and to the possibility of defying or escaping its worst oppressions. How that trajectory might have been continued had not syphilis and its associated afflictions put an end to his life we cannot know, but we can at least preserve the hope that there would have been no final capitulation of the kind recommended by Barbey d'Aurevilly and cravenly accepted by Sainte-Beuve's Amaury.

III.

THE CULT OF ARTIFICIALITY:

THE DEVELOPMENT OF DECADENT CONSCIOUSNESS

Having contemplated the brief account of his life and work given in the last chapter, it would be easy enough to feel sorry for Baudelaire. There is, however, a sense in which pity is out of place when contemplating the poets of Decadence. How, after all, could they have become poets of Decadence had they not been torn apart by the contradictions which others managed to avoid? If Baudelaire had not been denied his inheritance and forced to live on meager handouts disposed by a censorious guardian, how could he possibly have laid claim—as he did in the most celebrated of his four poems entitled "Spleen"—that he had more memories than if he had lived a thousand years, crowded as secrets in his unhappy brain? How could he have likened himself to a graveyard churned about by worms of remorse? And how, if he had only harbored such feelings for brief intervals of alienation, could he possibly have learned to savor the sensation as elaborately as he did? If he had made a better living, he would probably have been only one more Romantic or Parnassian dilettante; as it was, he became the inspiration of a whole Decadent Movement.

Gautier's analysis of Decadence understandably concentrated on matters of style. As an outspoken advocate of art for art's sake he naturally paid more attention to matters of form than matters of representation. When he set out to define Baudelaire's Decadence, he did so in terms of the artificiality of its appearances: its decorativeness, its delicacy, its complexity, its willingness to entertain the supernatural, and its tendency to put extremes to the test of further extension. So far as those later writers who picked up the torch of Decadence were concerned, though, there was far more to Baudelaire's celebration of artificiality than mere mannerism.

It was Rousseau who provided French Romanticism with its fundamental philosophy, and hence with its distinctive flavor, but by the time the Romantic Movement picked up pace in France, Rousseau's ideas were already attended by the dark shadow of Sade. Rousseau had attacked the philosophers of progress and the champions of civilization by extolling the superior morality of Nature, but he had already been outstripped by a more radical opposition which embraced Nature precisely because it had no morality at all. Would-be dissenters from Rousseauesque Romanticism tended to accept Sade's subversion of Rousseau, but were not inclined to follow his example any further. What they did instead was to set up, in simultaneous opposition to both the philosophy of progress and Romantic cult of the natural, a cult of the artificial.

The proponents of this cult of artificiality were prepared to accept that the luxuries of civilization were indeed enervating, but they argued that such luxuries were nevertheless very succulent, and ought to be savored rather than denied. The cult's adherents had no faith at all in the kind of perpetual progress imagined by Condorcet, and were quite prepared to believe that Paris—like Rome before it—was heading for some kind of ignominious collapse into barbarism; but they proposed that the sensible response to that state of affairs was to make the most of the luxuries of civilization while they lasted, and to extract from ingenious artifice everything that it had to offer. This proposition was to become the foundation stone of the Decadent consciousness.

Before the Decadent Movement actually got under way in the 1880s, the pessimism which the Decadents were to embrace was given an increased measure of respectability by the philosophy of Schopenhauer, which was popularized in France by Théodule Ribot in 1874. Schopenhauer argues that the world contains so much more misfortune than joy that life is fundamentally unhappy, tolerable only because the Will to Live persistently deceives us with unrealistic hopes. The enlightened man, according to Schopenhauer, must replace this deceptive Will with an honest Idea, whose contemplation is fundamentally aesthetic. This philosophy seemed to French aesthetes to be a justification and a significant underlining of what Baudelaire had attempted and achieved; they were ready and willing to make Decadence a Schopenhauerian Idea.

As second-rate comedians are fond of pointing out, no one was ever hurt by a fall, however steep; it is the abrupt halt at the end that does all the damage. Since the invention of the parachute, in fact, it has been possible for the adventurously-inclined to make a sport out of free-falling, to savor the aesthetics of descent. This, in metaphorical terms, was the strategy of those artists we now call Decadent. They decided that in spite of (perhaps even because of) its obvious technological achievements, their imperially-ambitious society was in a state of irrevocable cultural decline. They saw no virtue in Romantic rebellion, however, electing instead minutely to explore and grandiloquently to advertise the peculiar aesthetics of cultural free-fall. Taking Baudelaire as their figurehead, they set out to develop a new manifesto not merely for art, but also for life.

* * * * * * *

Most of the key features of Decadent art have already been discussed at some length, but it may be as well to make a brief summary here. First and foremost, Decadent art is not representative; it does not desire to reflect the commonplace conceptions of "Life" or "Nature," which it despises and makes every attempt to demythologize. Decadent literature points instead the way to an opposite ideal, wherein life and nature would become entirely subject to every kind of clever artifice. Because this ideal is incapable of attainment in practice, Decadent literature is essentially pessimistic, and sometimes brutally horrific, but this makes it all the more ruthless in demolishing the pretensions of rival philosophies. It mocks these rivals mercilessly, taking delight in turning everything which is ordinarily taken for granted topsy-turvy.

Decadent art is rich in fantasies, and sympathetic to everything which encourages the cultivation of fantasy; it is for this reason that it is in favor of opium, hashish, and other psychotropics, even though it recognizes that such substances are ultimately mind-rotting and life-consuming. It applauds those who have sufficient power of imagination not to require artificial aids, but is prepared to take an intense clinical interest even in the most hazardous derangements of the senses.

Decadent art is ever eager to make its fantasies as gorgeous as possible, but its exponents know well enough that those who undertake Odysseys in Exotica will encounter all manner of chimeras. The Decadent artist, knowing the futility of taking refuge in the commonplace, desires to confront these chimeras, to see them clearly, even though no understanding of them or reconciliation with them is possible. He desires this, in part, because he has an avid hunger for sensation, which can sometimes override the overly simple distinctions which are normally drawn between the pleasant and the unpleasant; he knows that horror is a stimulant. But he desires it for another reason too, which is that he feels that there is some essential truth in horror: that the world is sick at heart, and that acceptance of that truth demands that even the most obvious of evils—pain, death, and disease—may require aesthetic re-evaluation, and at the very least deserve to be more thoroughly and conscientiously explored.

Decadent literature is, intrinsically and proudly, a literature of moral challenge; it is sceptical, cynical, and satirical. It recognizes that everyday morality does not work either in practical or in psychological terms, and is therefore a sham, but that ideal morality is—not necessarily unfortunately—unattainable. The moral of a Decadent prose-poem or *conte cruel*, if it has a moral at all, is likely to recommend that we should make the best compromises we can, recognize that they are compromises, and refuse to be ashamed of them. Decadent art is, however, dedicated to the smashing of icons and idols, and it is always ready to attack stern moralists of every stripe; it is fiercely intolerant of intolerance and revels in the paradoxicality of such a stance.

* * * * * * *

A Decadent lifestyle may be constructed and maintained by applying these artistic prescriptions to life itself. Although many Decadent artists maintained a careful separation between art and life, the most wholehearted of them made concerted attempts to convert the philosophy of their art into a set of actual beliefs and practices.

The wholehearted Decadent believes that faith in the implicit unity of mechanical and moral progress is misplaced. He does not believe that one more political revolution might make a better world, nor that one more industrial revolution might secure it. In general, he thinks, things will get steadily worse until the whole social edifice collapses and lets the barbarians in. He accepts that salvation from the world's decay is highly unlikely to be found even at the personal level. He admits that the quest for ideal love cannot succeed in the real world, partly because real individuals cannot compete with the marvellous phantoms of the masturbatory imagination, and partly because real people are not by nature loving and faithful. (Decadent cynicism, in fact, asserts that people are fundamentally duplicitous and ever ready to betray those whom they claim to love.)

The wholehearted Decadent also accepts that the seductive illusions offered by drugs like wine, hashish, and opium flatter only to deceive. He thus renounces all hope of finding paradise within intimate relationships, or even within oneself, as well as all hope of a future Utopia. He does acknowledge, however, that no matter how hollow the luxurious artifices of civilization are, a good deal of pleasure is to be found therein. He is therefore an unrepentant sensualist, albeit of a determinedly cynical kind. Such rewards as life has to offer the honest and sensitive man, in his view, are to be sought by means of a languid hedonism which is contemptuous of arbitrary and tyrannical rules of conduct and regretfully scornful of all higher aspirations.

The Decadent consciousness is not, of course, a happy state of mind. To call the wholehearted Decadent a "languid hedonist" should not be taken to imply that he seeks the trivial rewards of contentment. In fact, the sensations which he seeks are likely to be much sharper and stranger than any commonplace pleasures. The Decadent connoisseur puts such a high value on the intensity of sensation that he is really only interested in the most piquant—perhaps it would not be overstating the case to say the most painful—of pleasures. This is necessary because the comforts of civilization with which he is so careful to surround himself act as layers of insulation, and because his endless self-indulgence erodes his capacity to take pleasure from anything commonplace.

The true Decadent is the perpetual victim of an escalating scale of ills, whose labels are the key terms in the Decadent vocabulary and the great bugbears of Decadent rhetoric. The weakest form of this oppression is impuissance, which is—as Baudelaire observed in *La Fanfarlo*—little more than a kind of idleness, a mere incapacity to rouse oneself to constructive action. In time, though, impuissance ceases to manifest itself in mere listlessness and becomes ennui: a constant, heavy, and sullen world-weariness which is almost impossible to dispel, even for a moment. When ennui ceases to be merely deadening and becomes tortuous, it is transmuted into that spleen about which Baudelaire wrote four poems: a seething, bilious, and viperish subspecies of melancholy.

In the grip of these discomfiting disorders the Decadent personality tends to be thoroughly apathetic, but the Decadent sees his apathy not so much as a failing as a kind of curse visited upon him by the conditions in which he must live. If it is to be reckoned as a kind of sin—we must remember that what we nowadays regard as a medical condition and call "clinical depression" used to be seen by the Catholic Church as the sin of *accidie*—then it is a sin from which conventional morality offers no hope of redemption. If the flame of his ashen spirit is to be reignited, and decadent man must have recourse not merely to new sensations but also to more dangerous sensations. His quest among the artificial paradises of the imagination is no idle daydreaming; it requires a fierce intensity of engagement. In addition to wine, opium, and hashish, he is likely to indulge in much more toxic stimulants like absinthe and ether. He remains, meanwhile, all too well aware that the greatest artifice of all, and by far the most promising, is Art; it is there, if anywhere, that there are victories to be won and triumphs to be deserved.

There is, of course, an inherent and ironic paradox in the fact that a creed which puts such a heavy emphasis on the comforts of artificiality proved to be desperately uncomfortable for all of its most fervent adherents. Many of the most wholehearted Decadents did indeed destroy themselves, aided by the scorn of their enemies; others set out more-or-less hastily on various roads to Damascus in search of magical renewals of faith which would restore the layers of spiritual insulation they had earlier discarded. While braver Decadents perished, the more cowardly relented, but either way a Decadent Movement could not help but be a short-lived affair.

History cannot offer us a single example of a thoroughly successful Decadent career, but this is hardly surprising, given that the philosophy of Decadence has so little room in it for success. It is almost *de rigeur* for a Decadent writer to die young, in miserable circumstances, before he can be considered seriously as a true champion of Decadent ideas. The work which the Decadents produced, however, contains a challenge to commonplace ideas of health, beauty, and goodness which deserves to be carefully weighed and taken seriously. Any idea for which people have been willing to mortify themselves deserves that much, even if one eventually comes to the conclusion that they were fools to do it.

* * * * * * *

Not all the writers we nowadays think of as Decadents conformed closely to the ideal type described above, and one would hard pressed to think of any who conformed to it in every single particular and never strayed outside its limits. There have been many temporary dabblers in Decadent consciousness and Decadent lifestyle, especially in times and places when such notions have become briefly fashionable. There have also been many careful experimenters whose adventures in Decadent style sit alongside other stylistic experiments and find little or no echo in the private lives of the experimenters. There have, of course, been very many men who indulged Decadent lifestyles to the extent that they never produced a single worthwhile Decadent work of art. The extent to which writers do resemble this type, however—first and foremost in the advocacy of their work, but also in the lives whose experience fuelled their artistry—is the extent to which they are worthy of the title of Decadent.

Any attempt to summarize the literary history of Decadence after Baudelaire inevitably runs into acute problems of delineation. There was a definite self-defined Decadent Movement in France in the late 1880s and a short-lived echo of it in England in the 1890s, but there are many other writers, some of whose work, although it falls outside these formally-identified movements, is definitely Decadent to some degree. Some of these writers were prepared to accept the label, some were anxious to avoid it, and some remained blissfully unaware of its possible relevance. Dozens, if not hundreds, of candidates for the dubious honor of being considered Decadent have been identified by critics and historians whose rules of definition vary considerably.

The situation is further confused by the fact that Decadent literature overlaps several other genres and movements, and that many of its key works can equally well be discussed under other labels. Many of the members of the French Decadent Movement were interested in the techniques of Symbolism, and many later critics preferred to discuss their work under that heading. Others were on the fringes of Naturalism, espousing a cynical and rather grotesque version of seedy realism. A few may be numbered among the significant precursors or actual progenitors of Surrealism. The evolution of literature is an untidy business which is not conducive to the drawing of sharp categorical boundaries.

The history of the idea of Decadence is, of course, confused by the fact that there are some interesting literary accounts of the Decadent lifestyle which were set down, with horrified disapproval, by writers who were anything but Decadent in their own outlook. There were also writers who railed against the Decadence of contemporary society in the forlorn hope of helping to cure its malaise; these catalogues of complaint often include perceptive accounts of Decadent consciousness which might be reckoned all the more interesting by virtue of the fact that they offer a view from without rather than within.

Just as there are some novelists who raise the specter of Decadence merely to condemn it, so there are historians and critics who define and describe Decadent literature primarily in order to disparage it. Even when that is not the intention—as it certainly is not here—the careful elaboration of the Decadent worldview and the careful cataloguing of the ruined lives led by many of its possessors can seem rather dispiriting. It may, therefore, be worth emphasizing that a good deal of Decadent prose is exuberantly playful, and that some of it is very witty.

Many of the French writers who adopted the Decadent pose in the mid-'80s were content to wear it flippantly, as if it were a gaudy costume or a decorative mask. The Decadent style and the Decadent lifestyle were for some of their adherents a liberating kind of fantasy, which allowed them to escape from the direly uncomfortable straitjacket of conventional moral expectations. For some writers involved in the Decadent Movements, and for many of the dabblers who came after them, there was a delicious freedom in being able to celebrate infidelity instead of fidelity, lust instead of love, and idiosyncratic fantasy instead of sanctified desire.

The opportunity offered by the Decadent consciousness for the cultivation of a new intensity in art and life turned out, at least in some instances, to be dangerous, absurd, and ultimately self-defeating. It must be remembered, however, that people who formulate their lifestyles under the tyrannical pressure of social conformity, and others who try to transcend normality by embracing Romantic idealism or the philosophy of Progress, rarely succeed in reaping abundant rewards by means of their careful hedonism and patient orthodoxy.

* * * * * * *

Baudelaire was not the only important precursor of the Decadent Movement. The Movement may be regarded as the direct progeny of the two young men who published essays on his work in 1866, Mallarmé and Verlaine, but its roots extended much further than those two essays, and the writers who took up the cause in the 1880s had other important inspirations on which to draw.

Baudelaire was nearly contemporary with another writer who was to achieve posthumous notoriety with a series of striking poems in prose embodying a worldview even more flamboyantly perverse than his own. This was Isidore Ducasse, who died in 1870 at the age of twenty-four, having produced *Les Chants de Maldoror* under a pseudonym borrowed from a sensational novel by Eugène Sue: the Comte de Lautréamont. He also produced a small volume of aphoristic essays, misleadingly entitled *Poésies*, under his own name, but it was the rather belated distribution of *Les Chants de Maldoror* which allowed his reputation to build by slow degrees.

Although there is no coherent story to be found therein, *Maldoror* might easily be reckoned a novel rather than a sequence of "songs" in prose. Most of the passages are delivered in the first person by the eponymous anti-hero, an "extraordinary accident of fate" who discovers that—in frank defiance of Rousseau's Nature—he has been "born evil." Having discovered that other men, whatever their natural inclinations, only succeed in becoming cowardly, Maldoror sets out gleefully to fulfill his own potential for monstrousness. In the most memorable sequence of all, he watches a company of sharks harass the survivors of a shipwreck and then turn on one another; he lends assistance to the largest and most vicious of them, a female with which he then has sexual intercourse, in celebration of the fact that they are true soulmates.

How seriously Ducasse intended the work of the Comte de Lautréamont to be taken is unclear. The *Poésies* certainly take a very different view of the proprieties of literary work, but, in the same way that the Marquis de Sade's loud protestations that he was definitely not the author of *Justine* were merely part of the overall pantomime, its ritual expressions of repugnance may well have been part and parcel of the *Maldoror* myth.

* * * * * * *

Another writer contemporary with Baudelaire who attracted the admiration of the Decadent Movement and was retrospectively co-opted into it was Gérard de Nerval, a friend of Gautier's who was notorious for having strolled in the gardens of the Palais Royal leading a lobster on a leash of pale blue ribbon. Nerval eventually went insane and killed himself, but in the early stages of his disturbance he contrived to transmute his mental disorder into various literary forms.

The most notable of these products was perhaps the phantasmagorical novella *Aurélia* (1855), which was published posthumously in the year of Nerval's death. It takes to an extreme of strangeness his constant preoccupation with seductive females, which is similar in some ways to Gautier's, but not nearly so orderly. Gautier had little difficulty crystallizing his images of perfect desirability, even though he had to employ supernatural motifs in order to do it; Nerval's tales are much more dreamlike, rather more mysterious in spite of their relative mundanity. A year before his death Nerval issued an entire collection of prose and poetry addressed to a series of real and imaginary women, to whom he applied the designation *Les Filles du feu*—the "fire" in question being the heat of passion.

Nerval also published, in more settled times, an episodic account of his *Voyage en Orient* (1851), providing an account of his earlier adventures in Cairo and elsewhere which is shot through with an unashamedly prurient curiosity about the affairs of the slave market and the customs of the harem. This was to provide an exemplar for many later writers; the "journey to the East" became a kind of secular pilgrimage which all French poets hoped or expected to make (although many found, when they actually set off, that sea travel and foreign climes were no more agreeable to them than to poor Baudelaire).

Although *Voyage en Orient* was a popular book, Nerval's poetry was not assembled into a comprehensive collection until 1877, and it was not until the heyday of Decadence approached that it was widely read and widely appreciated. His most influential poems included a *supernaturaliste* group written, as he put it, *par désespoir*: a product of his developing mental disturbance which helped to lay the groundwork for the intense interest which the Decadents took in the relationship between genius and madness.

* * * * * * *

The inspiration lent to the Decadent Movement by Gustave Flaubert was considerable, but it derived from only one strand of his work. *Madame Bovary*, which was published in serial form in the months preceding the release of *Les Fleurs du mal*, made his reputation as a paragon of realism, but the novel on which he began work immediately thereafter was *Salammbô* (1862), which applies the techniques of he modern novel "to perpetuate a mirage." *Salammbô*'s reconstruction of lost Carthage in all its barbaric splendor stands at the head of a tradition of remarkably lush historical fantasies, some of which were associated with the Decadent Movement, if only peripherally: Jean Lombard's *L'Agonie* (1888) and *Byzance* (1890), Anatole France's *Thaïs* (1890), and Pierre Louÿs's *Aphrodite* (1896).

Even greater inspiration was provided to the Decadent Movement by the last novel Flaubert published during his lifetime: the phantasmagoric *La Tentation de Saint Antoine* (1874). Even in the version Flaubert published, this extended poem in prose, filled with magicians, chimeras, and *femmes fatales*, is a remarkable phantasmagoria. Had he not been persuaded to set aside the version he first wrote in 1848-49 and revised in 1856, he would have been a more important precursor by far, for the earlier version is considerably longer and even more lurid, concluding on a very different note, with the confused Saint Anthony still beset by the Devil's mocking laughter.

Posthumous publication of Flaubert's juvenilia revealed that he had long been preoccupied by the character of Satan, and that the first version of *La Tentation* had been the culmination of a series of exercises in literary Satanism begun in the 1830s, which includes "Rêve d'enfer" and the novella "Smarh." By 1874, however, Flaubert had retreated considerably from the tacit blasphemy of these earlier works, and his continuation of their themes in two of the *Trois contes* which he issued as a collection in 1877, is much more careful. "Hérodias" is a version of one of the Decadents' favorite tales—that of Salomé's seductive dance, and her demand that the head of John the Baptist should be her prize—but it labors under the handicap of a stultifying and thoroughly mature restraint. The first version of *La Tentation de Saint Antoine*, by contrast, reveals that the young Flaubert was the first master of the Decadent style, and that he came closer than his contemporary readers could have imagined to embracing a thoroughly Decadent consciousness.

* * * * * *

Stéphane Mallarmé had begun to write the poetry which would later be co-opted by the Decadent Movement even before Baudelaire died; *L'Après-midi d'un faune* was first written in 1865, although it did not reach print for some time.

Critics ambitious to disconnect the development of Symbolism from the disreputability of Decadence are wont to point out that Mallarmé had already begun to differentiate his work from Baudelaire's influence, rejecting the pursuit of sensation for a much cooler attitude, embodied in the dramatic poem *Hérodiade*, which he began in write in 1864. By 1868 he had formulated a curious aesthetic theory which looked to the essences of a Platonic world of Ideals for inspiration and attempted to use art as a means of reaching out towards them and capturing something of their flavor, if not their nature. This was not, however, the way he was seen by his contemporaries.

Mallarmé had contributed material to the 1866 and 1871 volumes of *Le Parnasse contemporain* and to a number of periodicals, but he had issued no collection of his works and was still virtually unknown in 1884, when Paul Verlaine included him among the "accursed poets" whose damnation was celebrated in *Les Poètes maudits*, and his friend Joris-Karl Huysmans took the trouble to put extravagant praise for his work into the mouth of Jean Des Esseintes, the protagonist of *A rebours*.

For a while, at least, Mallarmé was content to bathe in the light of this attention, producing works which paid more heed and gave more credit to sensations, including the enigmatic and misleadingly-titled poem, "Prose pour Des Esseintes." His first collection of poetry and prose-poetry, *Poésies*, was not issued until 1887; the extended second edition of 1899 was not issued until six moths after his death, although several volumes of selections from it were issued in the meantime, sometimes supplemented with new items.

Although his association with Decadence can be seen retrospectively as a sideline, or even as a digression from Mallarmé's lifelong quest to produce a Grand Oeuvre embracing a markedly different aesthetic philosophy, Mallarmé certainly seemed to the leading members of the Decadent Movement to be one of them, and perhaps the best of them all. He addressed elegies to a number of writers whose works he particularly admired, celebrating the fact that their work lived on, and these included most of the significant precursors of Decadent literature: Gautier, Baudelaire, Poe, Verlaine, and the composer Richard Wagner (who was, at least for a while, far better appreciated in France than in his native land). These too were collected and published during his lifetime, as *Divagations* (1897), while the Grand Oeuvre remained a mirage imprinted on his lonely eye—and one which, he was willing to suppose, would probably have been ignored by the public even if he had managed to complete it.

* * * * * * *

Given that Baudelaire, Ducasse, and Nerval all died prematurely, one might have expected to find many writers who were Baudelaire's contemporaries still alive and active when the Decadent Movement went into top gear in the mid-1880s, but even the bridges provided by Verlaine and Mallarmé can hardly be reckoned straight and sturdy. In the world of the visual arts, however, there was one man who began producing what later came to be recognized as quintessentially Decadent paintings even before Baudelaire published *Les Fleurs du mal*, and was still doing so while the Decadent Movement of the *fin de siècle* was beginning to peter out. This was Gustave Moreau.

Moreau's earliest work was done in 1852, and he was an exhibitor in the Salon of 1853. Although he soon developed an unfortunate habit of beginning work on huge and intricately-detailed paintings which he never managed to complete (many of which remaining hanging to this day in his studio, which was converted after his death in 1898 into a museum of his work), he quickly moved on to the subjects which were to preoccupy him throughout his career: scenes taken from mythology, in which violence and extraordinary eroticism are combined. The adventures of Jupiter among human women—for which the god adopted a number of exotic disguises—were a particular fascination of his.

A particular favorite of the Decadent Movement was Moreau's "Les Prétendants," which depicts the massacre of Penelope's suitors by an unobtrusive Ulysses while Athena, the goddess of reason, looks down from the kind of vivid splash of light usually associated with the

Blessed Virgin. This is the painting which Claudius Ethal sent the Duc de Fréneuse to see in Jean Lorrain's *Monsieur de Phocas*, in order that he might obtain a more comprehensive understanding of the Decadent worldview. Moreau was very fond of painting pictures of *femmes fatales*, and his images of such figures may be considered definitive. He did several derived from Flaubert's *La Tentation de Saint Antoine*, but his most famous by far are two classic depictions of Salomé which he did in the mid-1870s, nowadays usually known as "L'Apparition" and "The Dance of Salomé."

Moreau's were the visual images through which various key myths and literary works were filtered for the appreciation of the Decadent Movement. He was also to be the principal inspiration of all the other French and Belgian painters who associated themselves or were claimed as fellow travellers by the Decadent Movement, the most important among them being Jean Delville, Fernand Khnopff, Odilon Redon, Félicien Rops, and James Ensor. Moreau provided frontispieces for a number of Decadent works, and his followers—especially Khnopff and Rops—provided illustrations for many more.

* * * * * * *

The remaining contemporaries of Baudelaire who were later to become involved in the Decadent Movement were mostly involved at the time with the Parnassian Movement, which was likewise a reaction against Romanticism, but was more modest in its objections and seemed to some critics to be little more than a reversion to Classicism. The Parnassians were, indeed, preoccupied with the Classical era, making abundant use of mythological imagery in their works, but they shared with Baudelaire and his successors a fascination with decorative language and fantastic imagery. The founder of the first Parnassian journal, the *Revue fantaisiste* (launched in 1859), was Catulle Mendès, who was later to publish a history of the Parnassian Movement in 1884.

Like almost everyone else, Mendès was acquainted with Théophile Gautier, but Gautier's initial liking for him was thrown dramatically into reverse when Mendès married his daughter Judith. The fact that Gautier considered him an unsuitable husband might well have had something to do with his Jewish origins, but it was expressed in terms of stern disapproval of his rakish lifestyle; Gautier's fears in this regard were quickly justified when Judith failed to reform him, and the two eventually separated.

Mendès's Decadent fiction is best discussed in the context of the Movement, but it is worth noting here that it was Mendès's anthology *Le Parnasse contemporain* which first published in its first volume (in 1866) the sixteen additional poems which Baudelaire intended to add to the third edition of *Les Fleurs du mal*, as well as providing the first significant showcase of Mallarmé's work. It was this anthology which attracted the attention of the man who was ultimately to become the second great icon of Decadent consciousness: Rimbaud.

Like Baudelaire, Jean-Nicolas-Arthur Rimbaud, who was born in 1854, suffered a fatal break in his family relationships when he was six years old. His father deserted his mother, apparently declaring that he was unable any longer to tolerate the severity of her rectitude. Rimbaud too was to rebel against this smothering domestic tyranny, embracing the revolutionary ideas of his teacher Georges Izambard, and three times running away from school in 1870 and 1871. In between these excursions he spent his time in the school library reading the most scandalous texts available, including books on alchemy, witchcraft, and ritual magic as well as supposedly-indecent poetry and novels. He became vehemently and aggressively atheistic, and wrote angry poems in profusion.

In 1870 Rimbaud sent several poems to Théodore de Banville, who was then helping to select material for the second of the three volumes of *Le Parnasse contemporain* (it appeared in 1871, the third volume following in 1876). Rimbaud claimed in the accompanying letter to be seventeen, and he expressed his fervent desire to be a Parnassian. The poems were not accepted, and this rejection many have prompted him, early in 1871, to lay out in a letter to his teacher Paul Demeny a new "theory and philosophy" of literature. He attacked "egoists" and resolved to become a Promethean "seer" by means of a "long, prodigious, and rational disordering of the senses." Foremost among the heroes whom he now expected to follow and surpass was Baudelaire, who was in his estimation "the king of poets, a veritable God."

In 1871 Rimbaud sent some poems to Paul Verlaine, who had contributed eight poems to the 1866 volume of *Le Parnasse contemporain*. Verlaine, in one of the fits of reckless enthusiasm to which he was frequently subject, immediately summoned the young acolyte to a meeting and became fast friends with him—much to the disgust and discomfort of the in-laws with whom he and his heavily-pregnant eighteen-year-old wife were living.

Rimbaud and Verlaine became enthusiastically involved in a mutual disordering of their experience, which was certainly prodigious, though perhaps not so conspicuously rational. They drank absinthe and smoked hashish, and although both were later to deny in writing that there was anything sexual in their undoubtedly intimate liaison—well, they would say that, wouldn't they? The two men lived in England for a while, idling, quarrelling, and smoking opium in the dens of Limehouse, before their stormy relationship came to a head in Brussels in 1873, when a drunken Verlaine fired a pistol at his infuriating friend, wounding him in the hand. Despite Rimbaud's attempts to exonerate him from all blame for this intemperate act, Verlaine was imprisoned for two years.

Rimbaud made few attempts to publish his work, and in 1874 he decided to renounce literature completely. He responded one last time to an urgent summons from Verlaine following the latter's release from prison, but found the elder poet in the grip of a reignited passion for the Catholic faith and turned his back on him forever. He then undertook a much-interrupted but undoubtedly determined journey to the East, ending up in charge of a trading-post in Abyssinia. His life there ultimately proved too staid, and he attempted, unsuccessfully, to take up a career as a gun-runner and slave-trafficker. His adventures were finally cut short early in 1891 when he returned to France because a tumor on his leg necessitated that the limb be amputated; he did not survive the year and died in Marseilles while trying to return to Abyssinia.

Rimbaud found on his return to France that he had become famous in his native land during the period of his absence, thanks to Verlaine's inclusion of an essay on his work in *Les Poètes maudits*. This had been followed by belated publication in 1886 of his most notable works, *Illuminations* and *Une Saison en enfer* (his last work, written in 1873), which had been incorrectly advertised by Verlaine as "posthumous." He was, however, scornfully uninterested in the fame which had accrued to his name. The position which he had achieved as a central figure of the Decadent eighties was thus unwelcome as well as anachronistic, but the perverse irony of it seems entirely appropriate.

* * * * * * *

It was left to Paul Verlaine to become the parent of the actual Decadent Movement, his unworthiness to occupy that role made manifest by the fact that after his mad adventures with Rimbaud he had returned home to a life of relative respectability. In 1881 he produced a volume of poems called *Sagesse* which were redolent with the spirit of repentance and reform, including a sequence of ten sonnets detailing his communion with a censorious but forgiving God. Reconciliation with his wife had, however, proved impossible, and his resolution faltered; he lapsed by degrees into lachrymose dissolution, and his survey of the work of various "accursed poets" was presumably done in a spirit of maudlin regret rather than defiance; the works to which he referred, however, spoke in a markedly different tone.

Although certain phases of his life probably offer better exemplars of the Decadent consciousness than anything he actually wrote, it is sometimes argued that Verlaine's sonnet "Langueur," which appeared in the *Le Chat noir* in 1883, was the launching-pad for fashionable Decadence. Its opening lines—"I am the Empire at the end of its decline/Which awaits the Barbarians fair and tall/While composing acrostics in an idle scrawl/To which sad sunlight lends its golden shine"[1]—evokes Montesquieu's notion of imperial decadence as a metaphor, much as Baudelaire had done in the version of "Spleen" which begins, "I am like the king of some rainy country/rich yet impotent"; but it does so to signify an exhaustion in which no spark of defiance still smoulders. Had its admirers not been able to supply that spark for themselves it could not have launched anything.

In 1883 Verlaine was still little-known as a poet, although his *Poèmes saturniens* had appeared as long ago as 1866 (like most of his subsequent books its publication had been subsidized and its initial circulation very limited). The younger writers who used the café called Le Chat Noir as a base and called their periodical after it would surely have regarded him as a drunken failure had he not had the notoriety of his imprisonment to assist the glamour of his presence in their midst; as it was, though, publication of *Les Poètes maudits* in 1884 easily made up for the cravenness of *Sagesse*. It was this collection of essays, paired with Huysmans's novel-cum-essay *A rebours*, which provided the Decadent Movement with a ready-made set of heroes and exemplars.

Thanks to *Les Poètes maudits*, Verlaine managed to establish himself as an opinion-maker; circles of Decadent poets rapidly formed around and alongside him. New periodicals were issued to carry forward the crusade initiated in *Le Chat noir*, although *Le Décadent* itself, issued by Anatole Baju, did not appear until April 1886 and died a year later. Verlaine's contributions to such periodicals were reasonably prolific, but relentlessly mediocre.

Typically, Verlaine did not like being labelled Decadent. This was understandable, in view of his supposed reinvestment in religious faith, but he could do nothing to negate the image which he had acquired, and his actions continued to speak louder than his words. He was, in any case, happy to cash in on his new-found notoriety. He was invited to England by Arthur Symons, who organized a lecture tour for him, so that he could explain the principles of Decadent aesthetics to audiences up and down the land (who must have been a trifle disappointed by what they heard). His admirers arranged a pension for him in 1894, before the state grudgingly consented to assist in his support the following year—support which lasted only a few months before his death in 1896.

In the years which preceded the death which he had hastened by his many misadventures, Verlaine was frequently hospitalized, and he spent the rest of his time shacked up with aging prostitutes. He was, in in his way, a living testimony to the neurotic quality of some literary endeavors, but there can be little doubt that he was a Decadent only by default and by accident. Had he ever become a critical and financial success, he would never have taken the perverse delight in damnation that was forced upon him by the combination of obscurity and belated notoriety.

IV.

A REBOURS:

JORIS-KARL HUYSMANS AND THE DECADENT MANIFESTO

It is arguable that the first Decadent novel was Elémir Bourges's conscientiously lurid *Le Crépuscule des dieux* (1883), in which the evil mistress of an aristocrat of the Second Empire encourages his three children to taste the fruits of their inherited degeneracy, leading to an orgy of incest, murder, suicide, and traumatic insanity. Bourges's venture into Decadence was, however, a whim which he did not follow through; his novel undoubtedly influenced the Decadent novelists who came after him, but it was not the most important exemplar which they had in mind. A much more spectacular and much more original novel appeared the following year, alongside Verlaine's study of *Les Poètes maudits*, and immediately became the central document of the French Decadent Movement: the rock upon which the edifice of Decadent prose fiction was erected. This was, of course, Joris-Karl Huysmans's *A rebours*. As well as presenting a definitive personification of the Decadent consciousness, *A rebours* was the text which identified, explicated, and waxed enthusiastic about a whole literary tradition of Decadent poetry and prose, and provided that tradition with a much wider historical and aesthetic context. The text thus became a kind of handbook of Decadent taste, Decadent doctrine, and Decadent understanding, as well as an archetype of Decadent artwork.

A rebours became the Bible of would-be Decadents of all kinds: those who were inspired to artistic Decadence; those who aspired to a Decadent lifestyle; and those embarked upon a wholehearted combination of the two. It laid out an extraordinarily elaborate Decadent manifesto, instructing the acolytes of the new creed as to what to read, how to appreciate what they read, and how to pass cynical judgment on the affairs of a world which they were fully entitled to despise. It sent people forth on quests for new experience, and granted a philosophical license to all manner of self-indulgent fetishisms—all this in spite of the fact that it was, in essence, the pipe-dream of a humble clerk who held a position in, of all places, the Sûreté.

Huysmans had been writing for some years before producing *A rebours*, but had given no indication that such a book was in him. His early prose poems and sketches, collected in *Le Drageoir aux épices* (1874), showed little trace of Baudelairean influence, and his first novel, *Marthe, histoire d'une fille* (1876), had placed him alongside Zola and Edmond Goncourt as a Naturalist. In the literary world of Paris he must have seemed a slight and rather staid figure, although he made friends with several of the Decadents-to-be at the salon of Charles Buet, including Jean Lorrain and Rachilde, and he was also acquainted with Mallarmé, Barbey d'Aurevilly, and Villiers de L'Isle-Adam. This evolving pattern of friendships presumably encouraged his spectacular change of direction—and spectacular it was, for the book became an instant sensation.

A rebours was also the book which carried the Decadent doctrine beyond the boundaries of France and Belgium. Although it was not translated into English until 1922, when it appeared as *Against the Grain*, its notoriety in England and America was assured by the famous passage in Oscar Wilde's novel, *The Picture of Dorian Gray* (1891), which describes the profound effect of a mysterious "yellow book" upon the imagination of the young anti-hero. The book is not named in the passage, but its identity is unmistakable; were anyone in doubt, all possible confusion was cleared away when Wilde was asked to identify it at his trial and did so. The book's potential audience in the English-speaking world was necessarily more select than its audience in France, but even those who could not read it for themselves could hear the details of its creed from others, given extra glamour by its esotericism.

A rebours is a strange work, more of a meditation than a novel. It is an elaborate and intense character study of a minor nobleman named Jean Des Esseintes, providing a detailed account of an experiment in lifestyle which he undertakes in the hope of discovering the perfect *modus vivendi*. It describes and explains the furnishing of his house, the stocking of his library-shelves, the choice of artwork for his walls, and the pursuit of his various idiosyncratic hobbies.

Some of Des Esseintes's tastes and mannerisms are borrowed, tongue-in-cheek, from the most celebrated of contemporary Parisian men-about-town, Comte Robert de Montesquiou—whose apartments had been described to Huysmans by Mallarmé—but he should not be regarded as a caricature of that fashionable dandy. He is, in fact, essentially a wryly fantastic self-projection of the author, hypothetically granted effectively limitless wealth and the freedom to indulge any and all aesthetic whims. It must not be forgotten that he is in large measure a calculatedly clownish figure, but it should not be forgotten either that behind the mask of absurd affectation there is an unmistakable depth of feeling. The experiment which *A rebours* describes ends—as it is ironically foredoomed to do—in ignominious failure, but the underlying quest which motivates it reflects a genuine yearning. The catalogue of

Des Esseintes's follies and affectations is full of flamboyant jokes, but the gloss of humor cannot and does not attempt to conceal the authenticity of his petty hatreds and his splenetic rejections of normality.

From the very outset *A rebours* accepts that an uncompromisingly Decadent worldview cannot actually work as a practical philosophy of life, but it insists that the Decadent's view of life and art is far clearer, aesthetically and morally, than anything which passes for common sense or orthodox faith. Des Esseintes's pretensions are, when extrapolated to their logical extreme, admittedly and calculatedly ludicrous; but the distaste and disgust which he feels for those very different aspirations which are tacitly expressed in the state of the world as it is, and as it is in the process of becoming, carry an authentic critical bite. Self-mockery is an intrinsic element in the pose which Des Esseintes adopts—just as it was in the pose which his admirer Oscar Wilde adopted in real life—but the insincerity of his view of himself is merely the velvet glove which overlies the steely sincerity of his mockery of the world.

* * * * * * *

By the time the story told in *A rebours* begins, Des Esseintes's various debilities have forced him to give up the kinds of activity which most easily qualify as "Decadent" in the vulgar mind. He has finished with all his mistresses, having passed through the various phases of fascination which took him from the stage-door to the gutter in search of deeper depravities. He has concluded his experiments in "unnatural" passion and "perverse" pleasures. He never was able to get far with his experiments with drugs, because they unfortunately failed to transport him to paradisal dreams, merely causing him to vomit. His one desire at the outset of the text, therefore, is to isolate himself in comfortable surroundings, seeking solace in adequately-furnished privacy.

The story told by the novel, insofar as it is a story at all, is a curious kind of Robinsonade. What Des Esseintes is trying to do is to maroon himself, albeit in luxury, on a desert island. His mission is to surround himself with such delightful artifacts that his solitude will be infinitely preferable to any material contact with actual human beings. These artifacts must be chosen with the utmost care, so that his relationships with them will not merely replace but vastly improve upon those relationships with actual persons which he has determined to sever.

The relationships which Des Esseintes sets out to establish with his surroundings are still, in the most important sense, human relationships, even though they are not relationships with actual persons. He still craves contact with the minds of men, but he seeks to refine that contact into a particular kind of perfection by restricting himself to the finest works which the minds of men can produce: their finest books, their most gorgeous paintings, and all the other excellent products of the hothouse of human genius. It is no part of Des Esseintes's intention to remove himself from society in order to cultivate some mystical communion with God or Nature; he is definitely not that kind of hermit. In fact, Nature is what he loathes more than all else. He recognizes and acknowledges the contributions made by the heritage of natural ingenuity to the selectively-bred flowers and perfumes of which he is a connoisseur, but he knows full well that such blooms and fragrances are products of culture, crucially remolded by human artifice. He is in love with the exotic, and for him exoticism is the quintessential manifestation of human imagination and human artistry.

Des Esseintes's antipathy to the natural has as its entirely proper counterpart a similar antipathy to the realistic. He despises works of art which are representative, infinitely preferring those which reach out beyond the actual, seeking to transform and transcend ordinary experience rather than merely recapitulating it. This is one of the reasons why he hopes to find in the company of selected artifacts a sense of being at home which he has despaired of finding in the company of actual people. People are intrinsically ordinary, and there is something unavoidably tedious about their fleshly presence; it is only in their finest artwork that they really become worthwhile.

Given the nature of Des Esseintes's quest, it is hardly surprising that many of the chapters of *A rebours* are devoted to exhaustive accounts of the choice of color-schemes for his apartments, and of the authors which he admits to his library, and of the painters whose work he elects to hang on his walls. He occasionally devotes himself to extravagant indulgences of the imagination, especially when he goes out walking, but the only actual orgy described in the text is an olfactory one: a hyperbolically sensual account of an intoxicating riot of perfumes.

In furnishing his rooms, Des Esseintes desires to reconcile two seemingly-contradictory ends: comfort and escape. He desires that his home should become a perfect cocoon, protecting him from all the vicissitudes of life, but he desires also that it should be equipped with magic doorways which will admit him to rich and extraordinary experiences. By means of his collection of fishing-rods, his copy of Poe's *Narrative of Arthur Gordon Pym*, and his ability to provide all the appropriate odors, he expects to be able to reproduce the sensation of a long sea-voyage without actually needing to abandon his fireside. Only by artifice can the achievement of such a paradoxical miracle be hoped for; in reality, one would have to choose between ease and adventure. Des Esseintes's experiment is a bold attempt not merely to banish reality, but also to obliterate its limitations.

Because of their subservience to this complex ambition, Des Esseintes's tastes in art and literature are inevitably eccentric. Some of his declared passions may seem to the modern reader to be entirely expectable: his love of Moreau's painting and Wagner's music, his adulation of Baudelaire and Mallarmé, his liking for Villiers de L'Isle-Adam's *contes cruels*, and his preference for the later work of Verlaine over the earlier are all exactly what one would expect, in retrospect. We must remember, though, that these choices could not have seemed so obvious or so consistent in 1884. Our modern consciousness of Moreau as the Decadent painter and of Wagner as the Decadent composer is partly due to the fact that they were so designated by Des Esseintes, tied by him to the literary coat-tails of Baudelaire and Verlaine.

It is worth remembering, too, that the word "Decadence" is used by Des Esseintes not to refer to the intellectual heirs of Baudelaire, even though Gautier had long since licensed such a use of the term, but in a rather more pedantic sense, to refer specifically to the period of Rome's decline. Des Esseintes favors us at an early stage of his narrative with a careful explanation of his preference for the Latin writers of the Decadence—especially the bawdy satirists Petronius and Lucius Apuleius—over more fashionably earnest writers like Virgil and Horace; this particular essay extends into a lengthy account of mostly-forgotten writers of the early Christian era.

At a later point in the text Des Esseintes picks up the thread of this curious literary history again, excusing the fascination with various obscure Catholic apologists which he maintains in parallel with his far more intimate and far more intense relationship with the prose-poetry of Baudelaire (he considers the prose-poem to be the highest form of literary art). He speaks so highly of the prose-poetry of Mallarmé—who was not then a well-known or well-thought-of writer—that his comments became the basis for that poet's subsequent reputation.

Des Esseintes has no affection at all for the mainstream of Christian philosophy and doctrinal elaboration, but there is in early Catholic writers a delicate hint of colorful paganism which he finds attractive, and he opines that some later writers in that tradition have cultivated a visionary element which he can admire. This tradition, as identified and described by Des Esseintes, culminates in the work of Barbey d'Aurevilly, whom Des Esseintes deems to have turned his attention to the "Satanic" element in the human character—something which appears in its purest state in the fiction and philosophy of the Marquis de Sade.

Huysmans was later to carry forward this tradition himself, taking up where Barbey d'Aurevilly had left off. His fascinated-but-disapproving study of Satanism, *Là-bas* (1891), provided his second great literary success. The tradition was then to pass into the custody of Anatole France, who brought it in *Le Puits de Sainte Clare* (1895) and *La Révolte des anges* (1914) to a pitch of perfection of which Des Esseintes would surely have waxed rapturous. Ironically (and perhaps sadly), Huysmans's own fascination with Catholic lore encouraged him to yet another spectacular change of direction, and to the renewal of religious faith expressed in such works as *En route* (1895) and *La Cathé-drale* (1898).

* * * * * * *

When he was asked at his trial whether *A rebours* was a moral or an immoral book, Oscar Wilde declined to comment, deeming the question impertinent and irrelevant. In the introduction to *The Picture of Dorian Gray* he had, of course, already expressed the opinion that books could not in any sensible way be classified as moral or immoral, but only as well-written or badly-written. In fact, one of the themes of *A rebours* is the absurdity of certain moral judgments, and Des Esseintes is often at pains to dismiss and ridicule conventional ideas of immorality. This inevitably confuses the question of the morality of the text, and might easily be held to render the question unanswerable, but it is easy enough to see why conventional moralists found certain sections of it very shocking: Huysmans set out to achieve precisely that effect.

In one of the passages best calculated to shock Des Esseintes recalls an earlier experiment of his, in which he took a sixteen-year-old youth to a brothel and then paid in advance for the boy to return for a limited number of fortnightly visits. His motive for doing this, as he recalls explaining to the brothel-keeper, was to turn the boy into a murderer; he reasoned that giving the boy a taste for pleasures he could ill afford would inevitably drive him to robbery, in the course of which career he would ultimately be forced by necessity to turn to violence. His reflection is intensely ironic—he adds the observation that the boy let him down, never having been featured in the newspapers as the perpetrator of any horrible crime—but the real point of the story is contained in an afterword which construes it as a parable. What he was doing, Des Esseintes claims, was constructing an allegory of modern education, which takes great care to open the eyes of the poor and underprivileged to that which lies beyond their means, thus sharpening their sense of deprivation. For this reason, he observes, the processes of education which notionally aim at refinement actually have the effect of increasing suffering, envy, and hatred.

There is an element of black comedy about all of this, including the interpretation and the conclusion, and the text shows Des Esseintes instantly taking refuge from his bleak observation in an obscure Latin text, but the satirical challenge to our commonplace assumption is by no means ineffectual. A hundred years of universal education have certainly not brought about a universal refinement of taste or morality, and one could easily make out a plausible case for their having increased the pain of deprivation—and, in consequence, crime and violence—in exactly the way that Des Esseintes alleges.

46

At a later point in the text Des Esseintes mourns the apparent decline in the number of brothels in Paris and the corresponding increase in the number of drinking-dens. He argues that there is in fact no difference between whores and barmaids, save that a man's relationships with the former are honestly artificial, whereas the latter carry an illusion of spontaneity; in either case the quest for sexual fulfillment has to be paid for, but the indirectness of the exchange which takes place in the tavern allows men to delude themselves that barmaids are conquests honorably won and that their favors are something freely given. His preference, needless to say, is for the honesty of the artifice rather than for the illusion—and in these observations too he finds a kind of allegory and a sign of the unfortunate way the world is going. Again, the passage is ironic, but again there is something in what he says, which still echoes today in a certain kind of feminist rhetoric which claims that prostitution is a more honest form of sexual commerce than marriage.

Another homiletic meditation is occasioned by the sight of street-urchins fighting savagely over a shoddy crust daubed with cheese and garlic. This causes Des Esseintes to ask his servant to prepare an equally-disgusting concoction in order that he can throw it into the arena, thus prolonging the fight and increasing its violence. He expresses the hope that this will clearly demonstrate to the boys exactly what kind of world they are living in and how they can expect it to serve them. While waiting for the snack to be prepared, Des Esseintes expresses his disgust at the appalling hypocrisy which suppresses contraception and abortion, and which makes such a virtue out of caring for orphan children while simultaneously guaranteeing that the lives for which they are saved will be savage and miserable. Again, this passage is essentially black comedy, but the force of its argument can hardly be ignored in a world which has been brought to the brink of ecocatastrophe by overpopulation, and in which those children who are dutifully "taken into care" in the most highly-developed nations are eventually expelled to live wild in the streets as muggers and rent-boys.

If we are asked, in the light of passages like this, to judge whether *A rebours* is a moral or an immoral book, we can only say that it depends whose morality we are considering, and how effective we deem dark sarcasm to be as a rhetorical strategy. Decadent moralizing is characteristically cast in an aggressively challenging mode which holds that nothing is unthinkable, and that much of what is ordinarily taken for granted is sicker than it seems.

* * * * * * *

The sardonic way of viewing the world which is displayed to such good effect in these little essays in cynical subversion is reflected in all Des Esseintes's evaluative inversions. He is an irredeemably sick man, and so he is ever anxious to find signs of sickness in events and trends which other people consider healthily progressive; by the same token, he is always on the lookout for ways to dignify sickness. He is concerned to point out, for instance, that the hothouse flowers whose beauty he appreciates so keenly are, in fact, frail and sickly by comparison with their natural counterparts and that their lovely delicacy can be regarded as a kind of induced disease. He waxes lyrical, too, on the subject of the way in which their patterns and colors may mimic the pallors and rashes symptomatic of human diseases.

With the aid of such analogies, Des Esseintes is desirous of constructing a new aesthetic philosophy, in which the morbid and the beautiful are categories which will overlap considerably, and perhaps come close to fusion. This is tacitly evident in the early chapter which deals with his taste in visual art, which encompasses not only Moreau's paintings of Salomé, but a series of engravings by Jan Luyken depicting the multitudinous tortures inflicted in the cause of religious persecution. It becomes much more explicit in the later chapters, which include his appraisals of such modern writers as his friend Villiers de L'Isle-Adam, the pioneer of the genre of *contes cruels*, and his beloved Baudelaire.

Baudelaire's great contribution to literature, according to Des Esseintes, had been to break a pattern by which *littérateurs* had devoted their attention to the ordinary virtues and vices, which could be expected to be part of the everyday course of human affairs. Earlier writers had, he admitted, sometimes studied conventional monomanias like ambition or avarice, but in general their labors were analogous to those of botanists who restricted their attention to common wild flowers in their ordinary habitats. Baudelaire, by contrast, dove into the murkiest depths of the soul, to the breeding-grounds of the truly interesting intellectual aberrations and moral diseases, to the psychological hothouses where ennui and spleen brought forth the most gorgeously warped blossoming of desire and fascination.

In arguing thus, Huysmans's hero sounded a clarion call for others to do likewise. He laid the ideative groundwork for a new generation of writers who would be unafraid to explore the possible horizons of human derangement. He demanded literary equivalents of the rarest and strangest hybrid flowers, and of the most exotic and intoxicating perfumes. He asked for a literature replete with artificiality, strangeness, and delicacy, whose appearances might easily be seen as analogous to the symptoms of disease, in which traditional aesthetic and moral judgments would be casually inverted: a literature of baroque prose poetry and fabulous *contes cruels*. This was what the writers associated with the Decadent Movements in France and England set out to produce.

The last and oddest of all Des Esseintes's inversions of normal expectation is the result of the failure of all previous remedies prescribed by his doctor to halt his slow decline. The idea itself arises out of a mistake he makes in passing on a prescription written by his doctor to his servant without glancing at it, assuming (wrongly) that it is a recipe for an enema. In fact, the doctor had specified a strength-building diet, but the perverse propriety of taking nourishment into the alimentary canal from the end opposite to that intended by nature is instantly recognized and warmly welcomed by the patient. Having become unable to obtain much nourishment from food or medicine taken by mouth, Des Esseintes derives real as well as aesthetic benefits as soon as he begins to take his sustenance by enema. He rejoices in the fact that although his stomach has always been so unaccommodating that he has never had the chance to become a gourmet, the culinary arts have at last been opened to the expression of his genius, and he sets out to plan his menus with enthusiasm.

This new dietary regime is so successful that for a while Des Esseintes believes that he is on the road to recovery, but he is not. At the end of the day, he simply is not fitted for the life he has tried so hard to adopt; like the ill-fated tortoise whose shell he decorates with jewels in an earlier chapter, he cannot bear the aesthetic intensity of his environment, and he knows that if he extends his experiment any further he is doomed to die.

The doctor's final and most brutal prognosis is that Des Esseintes must abandon his experiment and return to the society of his fellow men, or face imminent madness, consumption, and death. Des Esseintes—who is, of course, unable to share the modern reader's ready recognition that the doctor is a hopeless quack—is thrown into a quandary, believing the warning but hating the suggested remedy. The pressure of this awkward dilemma forces him to discover a suitably eccentric compromise: he is drawn to the idea of becoming a monk, thus continuing his seclusion within a community of recluses. He admits that he cannot take the Church very seriously, because of the way in which it has devalued itself by cheapening and compromising all its own ideals—most of which were wrong in the first place—but he can see no alternative.

Fortunately, there is in the end one thing which can and does serve for Des Esseintes as a perfect justification of religious faith, and that is the sheer impossibility of what that faith requires him to accept. In this view, faith becomes one more grandiose and fanciful product of human artifice, tolerable by virtue of its overblown absurdity.

* * * * * * *

All Huysmans's later novels have as their hero a man named Durtal, who seems a more realistic projection of the author than Jean Des Esseintes. Durtal's career ran so closely parallel to that of his maker that many readers have interpreted the novels as attempts at self-explanation and self-justification on the part of the author.

In *Là-bas* Durtal is a scholar who has decided to write a biography of Gilles de Rais, the French Marshal briefly associated with Joan of Arc, who had been the subject of a famous sorcery trial in 1440. His friend des Hermies is delighted that Durtal has abandoned the realist novel, but Durtal does not see his decision in quite the same way; he still sees himself as a Zolaesque Naturalist working in quasi-scientific manner to reveal and explain the wellsprings of human motivation. His methodology is explicitly modelled on that of Jules Michelet, who had transposed the literary Satanism of Baudelaire's litany to Satan into the realm of scholarly fantasy in *La Sorcière* (1862). Just as Michelet had placed himself imaginatively in the shoes of the victims of the Medieval witch-hunt in order to arrive at a new understanding of their alleged rebellion against the Church, so Durtal intends to use his own powers of empathy to understand how Gilles de Rais came to commit the crimes outlined in the confession which his accusers eventually persuaded him to sign.

Des Hermies introduces Durtal to the devout bell-ringer Louis Carhaix, whose occupation and close association with the symbols of Christian faith place him far above the corruption of contemporary Parisian life. It is to des Hermies and Carhaix that Durtal relates his interpretation of de Rais's career, and with whom he discusses its relevance to the modern world. Des Hermies assures Durtal that an unbroken tradition of Satanism extends from de Rais to contemporary Paris, and supplies him with research materials supporting this contention, but it is Hyacinthe Chantelouve—the wife of the historian at whose house he had first met des Hermies—who eventually takes Durtal to see a Black Mass after she has become his lover. Another of Durtal's informants is the astrologer Gévingey, with whom he discusses Spiritualism and the kinds of demon called incubi and succubi. It is through Gévingey rather than Madame Chantelouve that most of the information about the celebrant of the Black Mass, Canon Docre, is filtered; Gévingey has only recently been liberated from Docre's evil spell by the virtuous magician Dr. Johannès.

In their final discussion of matters raised by Durtal's investigations of the past and the present, des Hermies readily admits that he remains uneasily sceptical about the power of magic. Durtal agrees with him, and confesses that he is envious of Carhaix's committed faith, which allows him to believe that good will ultimately triumph over evil. All three men agree that the civilized world is moving to a sadly ignominious end beneath the dismal light of "storm-clouds of foul abomination"; only Carhaix can conserve any hope for the future, in his vision of an imminent miraculous return of the Holy Spirit.

Durtal's flirtation with Satanism and Madame Chantelouve is distinctly half-hearted in spite of its brief intensity. If Madame Chantelouve is indeed a vampiric succubus—as Durtal briefly suspects—she is a woefully inefficient one. In the end, the principal charge that Durtal brings against Satanism is not that it is evil, but merely that it is inefficient. This inefficiency is revealed not so much by the fact that Dr. Johannès has triumphed over Canon Docre in the war for Gévingey's soul, as by the fact that the visions of grandeur and exoticism which Satanism seems to offer have proved on actual inspection to be decidedly tawdry. When Durtal finally gets to see the Black Mass, he finds it sadly lacking in aesthetic excitement as well as demonic power. It is not sufficiently impressive to impose itself upon his imagination, and its failure dispels the erotic illusion which briefly bound him to Madame Chantelouve, allowing him to discard her.

Many commentators have, of course, regarded *Là-bas* as a *roman à clef*. Huysmans did involve himself for some time with Berthe Courrière, an enthusiastic acolyte of Joséphin Péladan, a would-be Rosicrucian magus who had inherited the mantle of the self-styled Eliphas Lévi (Alphonse Louis Constant). Péladan loved to pose as a great scholar-magician, and he was acquainted with Joseph-Antoine Boullan, an unfrocked priest who was the leading light of a curious heretical cult. Huysmans encouraged the supposition that he had taken these researches seriously by contributing a determinedly straight-faced preface to Jules Bois's scholarly fantasy *La Satanisme et la magie* (1895), most of whose "evidence" was taken from *Là-bas*. Whether he ever saw a Black Mass while he was touring the occult underworld of Paris with Berthe Courrière is, however, doubtful.

Although there was no shortage of would-be magicians in Paris during the late 1880s, actual Satan-worship was (as it always had been and still remains) a product of the lurid fantasies of the devout rather than the active practices of the unholy. Péladan and Boullan—like almost all other lifestyle fantasists who posed as magicians—placed themselves ostentatiously on the side of virtue, and only went on at such great lengths about the Satanist enemy in the hope of making their magical opposition to that enemy's supposed activities seem something more than an idiotic affectation. Péladan was also a prolific novelist who complained endlessly and in great detail about the Decadence of contemporary Paris, for which he recommended investment in his own unorthodox faith as the only effective cure.

The overwhelming probability, of course, is that Gilles de Rais was innocent; like all the other victims of famous sorcery trials he was framed by his enemies, who used the same vicious slanders to discredit and destroy him as the English had earlier used to discredit and destroy his companion-in-arms, Joan of Arc. Because his trial was a domestic affair, later generations of Frenchmen were content to let his conviction stand so that the Church might use it as a terrible example to those who faltered in the faith. The success of *Là-bas* as a scare-story is an ironic testament to the effectiveness of that kind of imaginative terrorism.

* * * * * * *

It is significant that the fights of fancy upon which Durtal and his two friends continually embark in *Là-bas* are forever being brought down to earth by the kindly attentions of Madame Carhaix, who is always bustling around with supplies of hot food. She, rather than the devout bell-ringer, is the novel's paragon of common sense and virtue; her unobtrusive presence within the plot is testimony to the fact that Huysmans never lost touch with reality while he was in pursuit of his temporary obsession.

Durtal's conclusion that Gilles de Rais was eventually driven to madness and remorse by the knowledge that there were no further depths of evil to be plumbed is a fantasization. It is, of course, closely akin to Michelet's fantasization of the witch-cult as an active imaginative rebellion against the tyranny of the Church, although it credits a deeper sincerity to Gilles de Rais. Both fantasies were formed by the device of placing a thoroughly modern Decadent consciousness in a situation to which it could not properly belong. Like Michelet, Huysmans surely knew that his "reconstruction" of Gilles de Rais's actions and motives was a fantasy, but he probably considered that to be irrelevant; he was, after all, writing a philosophical novel debating the status and worth of religious faith in the decadent Paris of the 1890s, not a history book.

Like the conclusion of *A rebours*, the conclusion of *Là-bas* casts some doubt on the wholeheartedness, if not the sincerity, of the reversion to more orthodox religious involvement which claimed both Durtal and Huysmans. Devout commentators have always wanted to see that relapse as a triumphant abandonment of the scepticism which prevented Durtal from embracing the hopeful faith of Louis Carhaix, but critics sympathetic to the Decadent manifesto naturally prefer to take a different view.

En route describes Durtal's life in a Trappist monastery. *La Cathédrale* chronicles his attachment to Chartres Cathedral. The latter book is so painstakingly researched, and the results of its researches so carefully laid out, that it still has some value as a guide-book to the edifice in question. *L'Oblat* (1903), which describes Durtal's novitiate in a Benedictine monastery, completes the cycle. In life as in his fiction Huysmans had by then—to all outward appearances, at least—reinvested utterly in the faith of his youth. He died in 1907, at the age of fifty-nine; the immediate cause of his death was cancer. Barbey d'Aurevilly's remark that the only way for the man who had written *Les Fleurs du mal* to avoid suicide was to return to the foot of the cross has been applied by many subsequent observers to Huysmans, but there is another interpretation which can be put upon the capitulation in question. Huysmans's reacceptance of the Catholic faith need not be seen as a terrible betrayal of the ideals of *A rebours* if the fate of Des Esseintes is properly understood.

It is the exoticism—both stylistic and thematic—of ideas which appeals to the true Decadent. It is the escapist potential of art which he values above all others: its capacity to act as a magical doorway which can take him, if only in the imagination, "anywhere out of the world"— which is where he desperately desires, and perhaps needs, to go. Des Esseintes realizes in the end that religious faith can provide a similar outlet, and that committed belief in the immortality of the soul can be viewed as a heroic dalliance with the ultimate absurdity. Perhaps that was the spirit in which Durtal—and Huysmans—embraced the faith; if so, the decision must be regarded as a clever extrapolation of glorious perversity rather than a meek renunciation of it.

For the Decadent, who loathes both Nature and realism, the fantastic idea of a life beyond death is attractive, because rather than in spite of the fact that he cannot sensibly believe in any such eventuality. It is precisely the fact that the hopeful belief in the immortality of the soul is a frail, sickly thing—easily regarded as a species of insanity— that requires the true Decadent to take it seriously, and to hang on to it when all else is gone. After all, what other guiding light can there possibility be for a man who is sick in body, sick in mind, and sick at heart, and for whom all material prescriptions have inevitably failed?

V.

EXTRAORDINARY SENSATIONS:

DISEASE, DISORDER, AND DECADENCE

The first thing the reader is told about Jean Des Esseintes in *A rebours*, and the key to his entire enterprise, is that he is sick: sick in body, sick in mind, and sick at heart. In accordance with the half-baked protoscience of the day, Huysmans echoes Edgar Allan Poe in attributing the foundations of this sickness to hereditary degeneracy. Aristocratic inbreeding and generations of cossetting have supposedly made each of Des Esseintes's forefathers more effete than his predecessor.

The idea that the bloodline associated with a particular name or title undergoes a slow enfeeblement with the passage of time can be seen as a corollary of the notion that cultures inevitably suffer a gradual decay from their peak of virility to their ignominious collapse. In both cases the analogy of the individual human lifespan is being applied on a larger scale. We know now, of course, that such analogies are false, but they are nevertheless tempting, and it is not surprising that they should have been so widely credited. Rome was not the only example of relevance to this particular application of the argument; it was widely believed that the pharaohs of ancient Egypt had followed a policy of inbreeding in order that their royal blood should not be diluted and had suffered a dramatic enfeeblement in consequence.

The attitude of Decadent writers to this kind of "hereditary degeneracy" is—as might be expected—complicated by a certain ambivalence. Indeed, their whole attitude to disease is distinctly odd, and it is perhaps the hardest aspect of their work for a modern reader to understand. It is sometimes difficult to remember that modern medicine is a very recent invention, and even more difficult to calculate the attitudes of mind which the prior situation engendered.

The Decadent Movement flourished at a time when there were no effective anti-bacterial agents and when the commonly-prescribed pain-killers and sleeping-draughts were opium derivatives. Its members lived in a world where people might suffer recurrent fevers throughout their lives, which might easily bring on hallucinations if untreated and almost certainly would if dosed with the available drugs. They lived in a world in which people who contracted tuberculosis—a very common disease among the city underclass—would simply fade away by degrees, becoming thin and hollow-eyed. They lived in a world, too, in which venereal disease was running riot, in which anyone who led a mildly dissolute life was likely to end up with syphilis. The medical "wisdom" of the day prescribed that syphilis should be treated by hopefully-selective poisoning of the affected organs with mercury, the logic of this treatment deriving from Paracelsus, who had reasoned that because syphilis as a product of the marketplace it ought to yield to propitiation of the metal named after the god of the marketplace, Mercury.

There are, of course, several possible reactions to such a state of worldly affairs. One is puritanism: the insistence that sexual relations should be so narrowly confined by morality as to prevent the possibility of infection. For those who find such a policy impossible or uncongenial, however—not to mention those for whom it has failed, one way or another—some process of mental accommodation is necessary. Baudelaire's determination to discover an aesthetic fascination in "the phosphorescence of putrescence" might seem to modern readers to be slightly sick in itself, but it may also be regarded as a bold attempt to salvage something of value from a situation that was both impossible and dreadful.

Given the limitations of contemporary medical science, it is easy to understand why Huysmans cannot say very clearly what the causes of Des Esseintes's sickness are. Indeed, the doctor is vague enough in his diagnoses to permit the interpretation that most, if not all, of Des Esseintes's actual symptoms are psychosomatic. It is, however, far more likely that his ills are to be attributed by the gradual progression of a syphilitic infection. Des Esseintes certainly seems to believe this, although the expressions of his conviction within the text are rather oblique.

* * * * * * *

In what is perhaps the most striking and most memorable chapter of *A rebours*, Des Esseintes takes delivery of the plants with which he intends to stock his conservatory. He has, of course, scorned all the kinds of flowers favored by common-or-garden horticulturalists in favor of various carnivorous plants and other freakish monsters. When he has arranged this "tidal wave of vegetation" he steps back to survey his creation, delighted by the fact that none of them look quite real, and that when Nature has not imitated human artifice she has borrowed "the vivid hues of...putrescent flesh and the hideous splendors of gangrene." He realizes that one particular group boasts markings which simulate the stigmata of syphilis.

He had a sudden vision, then, of humankind in its entirety, ceaselessly tormented since time immemorial by that contagion. From the beginning of the world, all living creatures had handed down from father to son the everlasting heritage: the eternal malady which had ravaged the ancestors of man, whose disfigurations could be seen on the recently-exhumed bones of the most ancient fossils! Without ever weakening in its destructive power it had descended through the centuries to the present day, cunningly concealing itself in all manner of painful disguises, in migraines and bronchial infections, hysterias and gouts. From time to time it clambered to the surface, preferentially assaulting those who were badly cared for and malnourished, exploding in lesions like nuggets of gold, ironically crowning the poor devils in its grip with diamond-studded head-dresses, compounding their misery by imprinting upon their skin the image of wealth and well-being.[1]

The waking vision ends here, but there is another to come; when Des Esseintes retires to bed, tired by his excitement, he is gripped by a bizarre nightmare, which confronts him with the incarnate specter of the "Great Plague": a horridly diseased rider. He flees, and eventually finds himself confronted with a woman who undergoes a progressive metamorphosis, the parts of her body being replaced and consumed by aspects of the plants he has earlier been studying. The text declares that "His obsessive reasoning persisted even in his nightmare, drawing an analogy between vegetation and infection." At the climax of the dream, he sees the woman's sexual organs as a huge Venus fly-trap: a "bloody maw surrounded by sword-blades"; a vegetal *vagina dentata*.[2]

If the reader takes these visions seriously, as he is surely intended to do, the physical basis of Des Esseintes's ills is clearly revealed therein. It is, of course, true that the slow and very variable phases of syphilis often mimic other diseases, throwing up a bewildering variety of symptoms which confuse the business of diagnosis and treatment. One consequence of this phenomenon is that a man might live for many years fearing—but never knowing for certain or ever being conclusively forced to admit to himself—that he might have that one dread disease rather than some unfortunate but marginally less horrible combination of others.

It was not actually necessary for a *fin-de-siècle* intellectual to catch syphilis in order to embrace the Decadent consciousness, but it certainly helped. These days, syphilis can be cured by a course of antibiotics; it had a very different existential significance in the days when there was no really effective treatment, and the standard prescription involved deliberate mercuric poisoning. In the 1880s an intimate understanding of the consequences of catching syphilis could not help but alter a man's attitude to the role of sexual passion in human affairs. Syphilis was a powerful antidote to the conventional mythology of love, and its afflictions could hardly help but blight a man's chances of finding contentment and fulfillment in marriage. It was also more difficult for the syphilitic than for the unafflicted man to maintain his faith in the fundamental benevolence of God; prayer and repentance were as unavailing in his case as mercury. The syphilitic of the 1880s was forced by his condition to be an outsider; he was already damned, perhaps to madness and delusion as well as premature death—and he had every reason to believe that the legacy of his own sins might indeed be visited upon his descendants.

* * * * * * *

Whether the mercury treatment had any effect at all on the development of syphilis is difficult to determine. No one has ever attempted a controlled experiment, and it would have been difficult to contrive an effective double blind even if they had. Perhaps the heavy-metal poisoning really did do more damage to the parasite than the host—but one thing we can be fairly sure of, now that we have catalogued the toxic effects of mercury more carefully, is that its own contribution to the derangement of the senses would be in the direction of stupidity rather than genius.

The mercury treatment was not the only quack cure which the members of the Decadent Movement had occasion to observe, and occasionally to endure. The only nineteenth-century "treatment" for tuberculosis which actually did any good was to remove the sufferer to a warmer and drier place, and the journeys to the East of which the Decadents thought so highly were often occasioned by the search for a more healthful climate. Sufferers for whom travel was impractical were, however, subject to a battery of supposedly-helpful suggestions, one of which was that it might help to consume considerable quantities of fresh ox-blood. Queues of feverish emaciates would form outside the abattoirs of Paris to claim this elixir while it was still warm.

The physiological effects of this treatment were unhelpful and dangerous, but the psychological effects of bearing witness to such commerce interested more than one Decadent writer. Rachilde's novel *La Marquise de Sade* (1887) did not quite reproduce the *succès de scandale* of her first venture into print, *Monsieur Vénus* (1884), but it offered a uniquely detailed account of the evolution of its heroine's thoroughly Decadent consciousness, which has its origin in the little girl's discovery of the full horror of the treatment which is being meted out to her sick mother. From that moment on, her sensibility—which is to say, the supposedly-natural inclination of her feelings to sympathy with her fellow beings—is crucially distorted, until she finally matures as a heartless connoisseur of cruelty.

The metaphorical potential of the treatment is subjected to more graphic extrapolation in "La Verre du sang" (1893) by Jean Lorrain (who probably tried the treatment himself in the hope of putting an end to his lifelong proneness to fevers). The doctors featured in this story inform an actress who is infatuated with a young girl that it is her own unnatural love which has afflicted the child with tuberculosis. The actress cannot bear to take her *protégée* to the abattoir herself, because the sight and stink of the blood makes her sick, but when the child returns from her ordeal with blood upon her lips, the kiss which the two exchange to celebrate their reunion makes the taste pleasurable.

Lorrain was one of the writers who waxed most lyrical about the strangely ethereal beauty which some sufferers from tuberculosis allegedly acquired. Like Huysmans he was also very fond of exploiting the symbolism of flowers. His career as a connoisseur of all things morbid will be discussed at greater length in Chapter VI, but it is worth calling attention here to the remarkable extent to which his life and his art were affected and afflicted by the combination of distressing illnesses and equally distressing treatments. When added to the testimony of Huysmans's *A rebours* and the relevant works of Octave Mirbeau—which are discussed in detail in Chapter VIII—Lorrain's accounts of the intricate interweaving of disease and moral disorder provide a vital key to the underlying and partly-hidden pathology of the Decadent consciousness.

The recent advent in our own world of AIDS should help us to understand how there came into being in the nineteenth century a worldview which the sick found easier to accept than the healthy. We ought to be able to understand well enough how it might have been the case that those who were forced to stand aside from the common run of human affairs thought themselves able—and perhaps were able—to look at the history and the lives of their fellow men more objectively, more clinically, and with more critical acumen than those who were still enmeshed by the drift-nets of normality.

Syphilis and tuberculosis, by virtue of their effects on the worldview of their more intellectually-inclined victims, must be reckoned to have been among the chief progenitors of the Decadent consciousness. This does not mean, however, that the Decadent philosophy was necessarily mistaken in its claim to offer us a clearer sight of the condition of the world than is contained in the self-satisfied illusions of the healthy man.

* * * * * * *

The medical science of the late nineteenth century seems to modern observers to have been a wilderness of ignorance, but it was not an empty wilderness. Much of what filled the void of knowledge was mere folly, but much of that folly was well-intentioned. Some of these follies—and the good intentions embodied therein—were of considerable importance to the way in which the Decadent philosophy attempted to save something worthwhile from the wreckage of disease and decay. Contemporary fashions in proto-psychology, with which many French writers of the nineteenth century kept in close touch, offered certain welcome endorsements to the Decadent pose, while quasi-scientific explorations of mind-altering drugs offered the possibility of access to imaginary worlds more interesting and more hospitable than disease-ridden actuality.

The experiments with hashish and opium which were undertaken by Théophile Gautier and other members of the self-styled Club de Hachischins in the 1830s and '40s were conducted in a spirit of exploration which had its scientific side. The drugs in question were often supplied by medical men who supposedly supervised and observed their use, and catalogued their effects. The doctor most closely involved with the hallucinatory adventures of Théophile Gautier and his friends was Joseph Moreau, who liked to style himself "Moreau de Tours." His study of *Hashish and Mental Alienation* (1845) was largely based in these experiments, and reprinted the whole of an article on "Hashish" which Gautier had published in 1843. The article describes Moreau as "an enthusiastic hashish eater," and observes that he took stronger doses of the drug than his companions.

Gautier's account of the effects of hashish has little in common with modern reports of the effects of cannabis. One is inclined to suspect, therefore, that the phenomena he describes have at least as much to do with his own expectations as with the physiological effects of the drug. This does not make them any less interesting, and may be held to increase their value as an account of what the experimenters were actually looking for when they set out upon their internal adventures.

Gautier recounts in his essay that he and his companons took hashish before consuming a meal, and that he retired once the plates had been cleared to a divan where he lay down "to await the ecstasy." His body then appeared to become transparent, allowing him to see the drug he had consumed as an emerald within his breast "emitting millions of little sparks." These began to spin around, joining with other precious stones in a kaleidoscopic dance. His companions now seemed to be disfigured, becoming chimerical figures with vegetal or avian characteristics. He began laughing and juggling with cushions. One of his companions spoke to him in Italian, which the hashish translated into Spanish—and yet "our conversation was almost rational and touched on everyday matters, gossip of the theatre or of literature."

The essay goes on to relate how Gautier, after a period of normality, experienced a second series of visions, involving swarms of butterflies and amazing flowers. His sense of hearing became so "acute" that he could "hear the very sounds of the colors" and was set adrift on an ocean of sounds. This brought him to the climax of his vision:

> Never had such beatitude flooded me with its waves: I had so melted into the indefinable, I was so absent, so free from myself (that detestable witness ever dogging one's footsteps) that I realised for the first time what might be the way of life of elemental spirits, of angels, and of souls separated from their bodies. I was like a sponge in the midst of the ocean: at every moment floods of happiness penetrated me.... my whole being had been transfused by the color of the medium into which I had been plunged.[3]

There is much here that anticipates the ambitions and visions which Huysmans credits to Jean Des Esseintes, and also much that anticipates the stories which Jean Lorrain was to write around his etherdreams; both writers must have been familiar with the essay and presumably used it as a source. To the extent that Lorrain's ether-dreams were subjectively-determined they may well have drawn upon expectations conditioned by Gautier's descriptions of his own hallucinatory experiences.

Baudelaire's essay which compares and contrasts the effects of wine and hashish, "Du vin et du hashish" (1851), is ostentatiously represented as a quasi-scientific study, its subtitle claiming that the two drugs are to be "compared as a means for the multiplication of the personality," but its tone is by no means clinical. The section of the essay which touches in the delights of alcoholic intoxication passes swiftly on to a sarcastic description of the "supersublime" ignominies of drunkenness; the briefer account of hashish follows much the same pattern.

Unlike Gautier, Baudelaire recommends that hashish be taken on an empty stomach, lest it should make the user vomit. He also advises that it one should submit oneself to its action only in "favorable circumstances and environments," because its effect is to magnify all subjective sensations, including the splenetic. His subsequent observations are more in tune with modern accounts of cannabis use—and are relayed from the viewpoint of a sober onlooker rather than one who has taken the drug—until he reaches a description of the "second phase" of effects, when the viewpoint switches to that of the user, and the phenomena described become suspiciously similar to those described in Gautier's essay. Once he has summarized Gautier's description, however, Baudelaire adds his own commentary:

> From time to time your personality vanishes. The sense of objectivity that creates pantheistical poets

and great actors becomes so powerful that you are confounded with external objects. Now you are a tree moaning in the wind and murmuring vegetal melodies to nature. Now you hover in the azure of an immensely expanded sky. Every sorrow has disappeared.... Soon the very idea of time will disappear. Occasionally, a brief interval of lucidity will supervene. You will find yourself coming out of a marvellous, fantastic world. You retain, in fact, the power of self-observation and on the morrow you will keep the memory of some of your sensations. But there is one mental faculty you cannot apply. I defy you to cut a pen or sharpen a pencil; that would be a task above your strength.[4]

The significance of the final bathetic remark, to a writer, is of course immense. Although Baudelaire goes on to speak approvingly of the kinds of sensory distortion which hashish permits, in respect of music and running water, he has already made his most damning criticism. The experiences in question cannot easily be transmuted into literary visions, at least in the short term—and once dreams have lost their immediacy they have lost almost all of their power of inspiration.

Unlike Gautier, Baudelaire describes a third phase of the action of the drug, when the user is possessed by megalomaniac feelings of superiority, which extends a certain feeling of well-being even to the next day's awakening—but it is a well-being which manifests itself as languor, as an incapacity for work. "This," Baudelaire adds, "is the well-deserved punishment of the impious prodigality with which you have squandered your nervous energy. You have cast your personality to the four winds and now you have painfully to reassemble and reconcentrate it."[5]

Baudelaire's conclusion, in this essay and in his later study of opium (borrowed in large measure from De Quincey's *Confessions of an English Opium-Eater*), is that an artist should not need psychotropic drugs to stimulate the imagination. The imagination ought to have the power to accomplish all that hashish will do—and more—while permitting the proper expression of the experiences in question. (It may be worth adding, although Baudelaire did not, that the imagination ought to have the power to accomplish all that real sexual intercourse can, in terms of vivid excitement, without carrying any danger of infection.)

Baudelaire's cautious conclusion undoubtedly seemed to some later Decadents to be an unnecessary quibble, and perhaps it seemed to others to be merely pusillanimous. For many who read it, the essence of his message was not its prudish pessimism regarding the usefulness of drugs, but rather its tacit acceptance that what the poetic imagination ought to be trying to achieve was exactly the kind of thing that Moreau de Tours and Gautier were trying to achieve by means of hashish: an escape into a different, more gorgeous, and altogether more glorious sense of being. Baudelaire might have poured cold water on the idea that psychotropic drugs offered a satisfactory means of going "anywhere out of the world," but he had conceded that their effect was indeed something of a route-map.

****

Joseph Moreau's interest in psychological phenomena was by no means confined to the study of psychotropic substances; he produced a whole series of books between 1835 and 1859 investigating the symptoms and alleged causes of "nervous disorders." His work exhibits two constant preoccupations which were of considerable potential interest to Decadents. The first was an intense interest in artistic genius as a species of neurosis; the second was a fascination with the alleged heredity of neurotic traits.

Moreau was by no means alone in these preoccupations, which were shared by several far more prestigious figures, most importantly the Italian physician Cesare Lombroso, whose book on the psychology of genius was translated into French at the height of the Decadent Movement, in 1884.

The emergent science of abnormal psychology was very heavily influenced by early evolutionist ideas, which made much of the contrary tendencies of "progress" and "degeneration" in searching for explanations of the palaeontological record. In France, of course, evolutionist thinking continued to be dominated by Lamarckian ideas—including the proposition that acquired characteristics could be inherited—for some years after the first publication in England (in 1859) of Darwin's ideas. As the human sciences came uneasily into being analogies were constantly drawn between society and biological organisms, so that the ills afflicting society could be explored by analogy with the pathology of disease.

It should be remembered that it was not merely individual diseases but the phenomenon of disease itself was not well-understood at this time; Pasteur did not develop the modern germ theory of disease until the 1860s, and a considerable confusion of medical and moral attitudes persisted for some time afterwards. The real and evident correlation between sexual license and venereal disease was echoed in protopsychology by dark superstitions regarding the effects of habitual masturbation, and no one could be sure exactly to what extent the sins of fathers might be visited upon their sons.

In consequence of speculations about the gradual loss of virility in families whose succeeding generations indulged themselves to the full in luxury and vice there emerged in the proto-psychology of nineteenth-century France and England a new medical myth: the myth of neurasthenia. The neurasthenic was a physically weak and over-sensitive individual, likely also to be morally weak, permanently possessed by apathy and spiritual impotence. His (or her—though females were more likely to be diagnosed as "hysteric") condition was primarily the result of bad hereditary, but could easily be inflamed by masturbation and other bad habits.

The closeness of this image to the image of the Decadent personality is by no means entirely coincidental; the pseudoscientific theorists of degeneracy fed upon literary inspiration, and returned what they had borrowed with generous interest. But the proto-psychologists went further than this, offering speculations which put the neurotic victim of bad heredity in a rather more romantic light. Moreau and Lombroso were both concerned to argue that artistic genius was itself a species of neurosis, closely associated with bad heredity and eccentric lifestyle. The unfortunate victims of neurasthenia were therefore offered a possible route to compensatory achievement; would-be Decadents were encouraged to believe that the madder and more miserable they were, the more justified they might be in thinking of themselves as men of genius.

* * * * * * *

The influence of proto-psychology was by no means confined to writers of a Decadent stripe; indeed, the French writer who was most elaborately influenced by theories of hereditary degeneracy was Émile Zola, whose extensive analysis of the family tree of the Rougon-Macquarts is firmly rooted in such ideas. Zola, like Sainte-Beuve before him, was writing about victims of bad heredity from what he believed to be a clinically objective standpoint. Zola saw himself as a "Naturalist" in a quasi-scientific sense as well as a literary sense, as did Edmond Goncourt, whose techniques of characterization were similarly "medicated" by association with contemporary theories of psychology and physiology.

It is not surprising that such authors as Zola and Goncourt were in no hurry to associate themselves more closely with their subject-matter; they were anxious to preserve their objectivity, if not to resist infection. Nor is it surprising, however, that others took a different view. Some were bold enough to profess themselves entirely content to be mad, bad, and dangerous to know, if such a condition were the red badge of courage which the authentic genius must wear.

With theories of the close relationship between genius and madness to guide them, would-be Decadents were sometimes prepared to take great pains to cultivate their neurasthenia, or at the very least to be conscientious hypochondriacs. They treasured their symptoms, not only as reflections of the unfortunate nature of the human condition, but also as evidences of their intellectual superiority over the common herd.

This absorption of the idea of Decadence into pseudopsychological theory became an important factor in the literary criticism which grew up alongside the movement. Paul Bourget, one of the most prestigious contemporary critics to dignify Decadent art with serious consideration and tentative approval, was one of several writers who used quasi-psychiatric analysis to weld philosophical, historical, and literary ideas of decadence together into a composite account of the predicament of modern man. His two series of *Essais de psychologie contemporaine* (1883, 1885) analyzed the supposed sickness of the age by reference to its great writers.

It was, inevitably, from his contemplation of Baudelaire that Bourget drew the theory of decadence which was to provide the first formal "explanation" of what the writers of the Decadent Movement were doing, and why it was culturally significant. Indeed, Bourget had attempted to revive interest in Baudelaire's work, with specific reference to "the terrible word decadence," in 1876, some years before Verlaine produced *Les Poètes maudits*. In 1878 Bourget produced a quasi-autobiographical novel in verse, *Edel*, which attempts analysis of a mind afflicted by spleen and melancholic frenzy, yearning for a means of escaping the deadening burden of reality even if the price to be paid might be madness. Shortly thereafter, he gave up working as a teacher in a private school and began supporting himself by his journalistic endeavors.

As well as keeping up with literary matters—he became a close friend of Barbey d'Aurevilly, Edmond Goncourt, and others in their circle—Bourget read widely in the overlapping fields of philosophy and social science, becoming fascinated by the ideas of the positivist historian Hippolyte Taine (who also wrote a history of English literature) and the psychologist Théodule Ribot, whose concept of "affective memory" was later taken up by Konstantin Stanislavsky as the basis of his acting method. When Bourget attempted to bring his various researches together into a single theoretical framework, his primary purpose was was to attempt a scientific analysis of exactly the same situation whose poetic analysis he had earlier attempted in *Edel*.

Civilization, Bourget argued in the *Essais*, had greatly exaggerated a fundamental disharmony between human desire and the reality of the world. In promising (and partly making good its promise) that men would be able to realize their desires, civilization had made their failure much harder to bear, thus increasing their unhappiness. At the same time, he proposed, civilization had—over many generations—sapped men's virility, leading the most advanced nations to a state of collective nervous exhaustion. The progress of science had in Bourget's estimation served only to increase the anguish stemming from these sources, by draining the poetry out of existence and devastating the religious faith which had consoled previous generations. Given all this, what recourse was there for a sensitive soul save to make desperate (but unfortunately doomed) attempts to escape to a more hospitable state of being?

By such argumentative means Bourget constructed an apologetic case for Baudelaire's Decadent consciousness as well as his Decadent style—a case which made him out to be a tragic hero, condemned to struggle nobly and bravely against circumstances far beyond his control. Such representations are always seductive, not merely because they credit the would-be Decadent with sensitivity, clear-sightedness, nobility, and courage, but also—and perhaps most importantly of all— because they absolve the artist of all personal responsibility for his failure to please his audience or live a satisfying life.

Inevitably, the kind of grand theorizing in which Bourget indulged could not be content with a handful of French writers as key exemplars; it had to demonstrate its universality by showing that there were kindred spirits in other civilized nations. Edgar Allan Poe was, of course, easily accommodated, and Bourget made pilgrimages to Britain to immerse himself in the heritage of Coleridge, De Quincey, and the Pre-Raphaelites, who thus came to be numbered among the significant antecedents and key influences on the French and English Decadent Movements. Theorists who followed in Bourget's footsteps cast their net ever more widely; angst-ridden Germanic pessimists and gloomy Russian nihilists were smoothly absorbed by later commentators into the expanding canon of literary Decadence, and so were those Italian writers who turned a jaundiced eye on the reduced circumstances of contemporary Rome.

Bourget's conflation of literary Decadence with proto-psychological accounts was taken to a further stage by Max Nordau in *Entartung* (1892), which was translated into French in 1894. Nordau made much of the notion of hereditary degeneracy, defining it as a physical and psychological condition whose mental symptoms include impuissance, moral failure, bad dreams, and mysticism. Nordau accepted Lombroso's dictum that genius is a form of neurosis, but he regarded this as an indictment of genius rather than a glorification of neurosis. When he issued a list of artists who were victims of degeneracy, he did so more in pity and disgust than in wonder or respect.

Nordau's list of degenerate artists is, of course, headed by Baudelaire, Verlaine, and Mallarmé, but it expands like Bourget's wide-cast net to take in figures from many other nations, including the English Pre-Raphaelites, Wagner, Ibsen, and Tolstoy (who had not yet written the fierce denunciation of all Decadent art—including his own early work—contained in his 1898 tract *What is Art?*). Far less flattering than its predecessors, Nordau's work was presumably less of an encouragement to lifestyle fantasists and might well have helped to damp down the enthusiasm that drove the Decadent Movement. For at least ten years, though, it was Paul Bourget's analysis of the Decadent predicament that held sway in Paris, and Bourget's admiration which flattered the egos of candidates for the laurels of Decadent genius.

PART TWO

CASE STUDIES FROM THE DECADENT MOVEMENT

VI.

MASQUES:

JEAN LORRAIN AND
THE DECADENT QUEST

Paul Alexandre Martin Duval was born in 1855 at Fécamp, a small seaside town in Normandy. He considered that he came from a good family, but it was not a noble one; his father, Amable Duval, was a ship-owner whose vessels were involved in trans-Atlantic trade, while his paternal grandfather and great-grandfather had captained similar vessels. Like them he was fair-haired, a trait which he attributed to Viking blood.

In later life, when he had become Jean Lorrain because his father did not want the good name of Duval to be trailed through the mud of a literary career, his feelings about his ancestry were mixed—as, indeed, were his feelings about everything else. On the one hand he was prepared to be proud of the blond taint of "barbarism," which set him apart from the effete snobs of Paris. On the other hand, like the scion of any family of parvenus, he was very conscious of the fact that he was not an aristocrat, and would never be fully accepted into the high social circles whose lifestyle and pretensions he desperately coveted. The fascinated loathing which he cultivated for the decadence of *fin de siècle* Paris has a good deal of envy and ardent desire in it; in the words of Hubert Juin, he "loved his epoch to the point of detestation."

Lorrain's love of fiction was fostered at an early age and fervently encouraged. He was exceptionally fond of fairy tales, fables, and fantasies, particularly fascinated by the idealized princesses who were so often their central characters. In later life he was to write many such *contes* himself, the vast majority of them featuring exotic princesses; his most important collection of them was issued under the title *Princesses d'ivoire et d'ivresse* (1902). He was also very fond of charades, and loved dressing up in silks and velvets.

Lorrain completed his schooling with the Dominicans, which served to confirm a contemptuous hatred for the clergy which was to last a lifetime. By this time he was something of an *enfant terrible*, but no novice in the art of notoriety could possibly compete with the local

English exiles, who had crossed the channel to avoid the fiercer strictures of Victorianism. Swinburne had lived nearby for some years and still remained the perfect model of notoriety so far as Fécamp was concerned. The exotically lurid décor of Swinburne's house, and the scandalous things which were rumored to go on there, remained common knowledge long after Swinburne had departed. Lorrain never had the chance to meet Swinburne, but he did encounter another exile, Lord Arthur Somerset, a great admirer of Oscar Wilde who was a colorful character in his own right. Lord Arthur maintained a correspondence with Lorrain for some time, sending him pictures by Walter Crane and Edward Burne-Jones by way of assisting his artistic education. One of Lorrain's most striking early stories—the title-story of the collection *Sonyeuse* (1891)—is a fantasy reminiscent of Poe, in which a young man from Fécamp encounters an exotic English exile, Lady Mordaunt, with bizarre consequences.

By far the most significant of Lorrain's encounters in Normandy was with Judith Gautier, whom he met while she was on holiday there in 1873. She was ten years older than he, still married to—but already separated from—Catulle Mendès. To her their brief acquaintance was a trivial matter—she made no mention of Lorrain in her autobiography—but he was profoundly affected by it. It changed his life to such an extent that Edmond Goncourt was later to lament that it had been the ruination of him, and that everything which happened to him after Judith Gautier's intervention was a long-drawn-out process of moral and physical suicide. Goncourt seems to have believed (falsely, one must presume) that Lorrain's homosexuality was some kind of traumatic response to his doomed infatuation with Judith.

When Lorrain had completed a year's military service, his father sent him to study law, but Lorrain soon began to suffer from burning fevers and chest-pains, probably caused by tuberculosis. He would suffer recurrent bouts of this trouble for the rest of his life. The fevers were fierce and debilitating, sometimes bad enough to require injections of morphine, but he never became a habitual user of the drug (his characterization of female "*morphinées*" in his later fiction is savagely scornful). His feelings regarding his illness were typically mixed; he knew that Swinburne had been a career invalid, and he insisted that his sickroom was appropriately decorated.

It cannot have come as a surprise to Amable Duval when his son announced that he was giving up the law in favor of a literary career; he agreed readily enough to provide a modest allowance, on condition that the family name was veiled by a pseudonym. In 1880 Lorrain set himself up in Montmartre, eager to launch himself into the Bohemian life. This was the Montmartre of Toulouse-Lautrec, a world of cheap furnished rooms in which impoverished members of the literary avant garde rubbed shoulders with cheap prostitutes and formed enthusiastic cliques in cafés. The café in which Jean Lorrain elected to spend

most of his days was Le Chat Noir. Its habitués—who included Jean
Moréas and Jean Richepin—were then in the habit of describing themselves as "Hydropathes" and "Zutistes" (although Moréas was later to
identify himself as a Decadent, and then as a Symbolist, before revert-
ing to classicism in later life). The Hydropathes were self-proclaimed
literary Satanists, great admirers of Jules Michelet and enthusiastic
apologists for anyone brave enough to employ Satan's name in opposition to the moral and intellectual tyranny of the Church. Many of the
poems Lorrain wrote under this influence are reprinted in *Sang des
dieux* (1882) and *La Forêt bleue* (1883). *Sang des dieux* had a fron-
tispiece by Gustave Moreau; Lorrain met the artist in 1880, and immediately became a devout admirer of his work.

Lorrain found in Moreau's work a new worldview: a gorgeous
symbolically-transfigured vision of a world dominated by *luxure* and
luxe (lust and luxury), where eroticism, situated in fabulously gaudy
settings, is inextricably linked with cruelty and death. The *femmes fatales* who dominated the hallucinatory world of Moreau's paintings—Salomé, Helen of Troy, the Sirens—seemed to Lorrain to be different incarnations of the same individual. In Flaubert's *La Tentation
de Saint Antoine*—which was another favorite of the Hydropathes as
well as a favorite source of inspiration for Moreau—the archetype of
this fascinating species is called Ennoïa, but Lorrain preferred to char-
acterize the ideal of hazardous lust as Astarté, the Phoenician goddess
of love. In his work, though, "she" had an understandable tendency to
become androgynous or frankly masculine.

* * * * * * *

In 1883 Lorrain began to frequent the salon of Charles Buet,
where he made three more highly significant acquaintances. The first
was Barbey d'Aurevilly, then in his seventies, but still recognized as
the leading exponent of the philosophy of "dandyism" (which he had
considerably transformed after borrowing the initial inspiration from
Beau Brummell).

Lorrain became such a wholehearted convert to dandyism that
Rémy de Gourmont was later to describe him as "the sole disciple of
Barbey d'Aurevilly," but he was always working from a position of irreparable disadvantage. Many of those who were already dandies were
of the opinion that one had to be born to the vocation, and that no matter how hard one tried to adopt the philosophy and the manners of a
dandy, one could never truly become one. Some of Lorrain's contemporaries were inclined to refer to him as "the poor man's Montesquiou," and it is hardly surprising that Lorrain cultivated a deep
loathing for the flamboyant Comte. Throughout his career as a chronicler of the *fin de siècle* Lorrain sniped at Montesquiou, often viciously,
but he could never win the undeclared war because Montesquiou auto-

matically adopted the perfect defense: he ignored Lorrain completely, refusing even to concede him the dignity of being noticed.

The second important acquaintance Lorrain made at Chez Charles Buet in 1883 was Huysmans, who was already working on *A rebours*. Lorrain's fourth collection of poetry, *Les Griseries* (1887), consists of material explicitly inspired by *A rebours*. Lorrain and Huysmans became good friends—a friendship which endured rather better than most of Lorrain's associations, although it was weakened when Huysmans turned to religion. Long after that, however, Huysmans wrote to Lorrain in order to heap praise upon *Monsieur de Phocas* (1901), recognizing both its close kinship with and its significant variations from *A rebours*.

The third, and by no means the least, of the friends Lorrain made through Buet was Marguerite Eymery, who only just begun calling herself Rachilde. Her literary career was yet to begin in earnest, although she had already begun to cultivate the notoriety which shaped her reputation. Rachilde shared Lorrain's passionate fascination for masked balls, which were then in their last period of great fashionability, and he became her regular escort, enthusiastically competing with her in the outrageousness of his costumes. The fact that he was openly homosexual made the liaison all the more useful in terms of her flair for self-publicity.

While he cultivated these acquaintances Lorrain was gradually making a name for himself with the vicious reviews which he wrote for the *Courrier français*, a successor to *Le Chat noir*. It was in the *Courrier* he first cultivated the scathing rhetoric for which he became famous. He attacked Zola, Maupassant, and—most vitriolically of all— Catulle Mendès, but he could be correspondingly enthusiastic about the things he liked, which included Bourges's *Le Crépuscule des dieux*, and, of course, *A rebours*. His article flamboyantly advertising Rachilde, "Madame Salamandre" (1884), became her launching-pad, cementing the scandalous success of *Monsieur Vénus*.

Lorrain and Rachilde drifted apart in the years following her marriage to Alfred Vallette, the staid editor of the *Mercure de France* (of whose work Lorrain was scornful), but they remained on good terms and she treated him far better than most of the other females upon whom he became asexually fixated.

The firmest of all the friends Lorrain made in Paris was Edmond Goncourt, whom he met in 1885. Goncourt was thirty-three years older than Lorrain, but this did not inhibit their friendship; they remained close until Goncourt's death in 1896. Goncourt always wrote about Lorrain in warm but sad terms, lamenting the tragedy of his having somehow gone wrong in life. He took the younger man under his wing, perhaps seeing something in him that reminded him of his younger brother and collaborator Jules, who had died in 1870.

71

In 1886 Lorrain met Sarah Bernhardt for the first time, and became one of the most fervent of her many admirers. She was the central figure of the Parisian *monde*, and she held the key to social acceptance in the circles in which Lorrain desperately desired to move. Her attitude to him was, however, one of amused tolerance. She accepted his adoration, but like Judith Gautier before her she much preferred the company of Pierre Loti and Robert de Montesquiou, his two *bêtes noires*. They were both as openly homosexual as Lorrain, but in the eyes of the world—or those people in it who really mattered—Lorrain could never match Loti for style or Montesquiou for breeding, and he never enjoyed the same degree of immunity from disapproval.

Lorrain wrote several plays whose main parts were tailor-made for Sarah Bernhardt, but she refused to appear in any of them. He continued to be extremely enthusiastic about her work, especially when she played male roles, but his patience finally broke. In 1900, when she had one of her greatest triumphs in Edmond Rostand's *L'Aiglon*, Lorrain attacked it with all the fury he could muster. Later, though, he was to use her as a model for characters in two of his more sentimental novels: Nora Lerys in *Ellen* (1906) and Linda in *Le Tréteau* (1906).

* * * * * * *

Amable Duval died in 1886, leaving his heirs to discover that his financial affairs were in poor order. The estate had to be liquidated in order to pay off his debts, which increased the cynical hatred that Lorrain already had for all things bourgeois, especially commerce and the law. His mother had kept complete control of her dowry, and was not impoverished, but the necessity for Lorrain to earn his own living was now acute. He threw himself into journalism with great determination, and increased his output of prose fiction considerably. He had already published his first novel, *Les Lépilliers* (1885), and he quickly followed it up with *Très Russe* (1886).

Lorrain's fiction was destined to make him at least as many enemies as his journalism, and Guy de Maupassant was sufficiently incensed by resemblances between himself and one of the characters in *Très Russe* to send his seconds round to seek reparation from the author. No one knows what passed between them, but no duel actually took place. This was the first of several such incidents. In 1887 Lorrain did go to meet the journalist René Maizeroy, but both came away unscathed. In 1888 Paul Verlaine sent his seconds round after Lorrain had erroneously reported that he had been committed to an insane asylum, but the matter went no further. The most famous of his duels was, however, still some way off.

In the short fiction which he now began to write prolifically Lorrain frequently introduced homosexual themes. Lesbianism had long been fashionable as a literary theme thanks to Baudelaire—who intended at one point to attach the title *Les Lesbiennes* to the collection which became *Les Fleurs du mal*—and to Gautier's *Mademoiselle de Maupin*, but male homosexuality was still hedged about with taboos. Lorrain was not displeased by the shock-waves generated by his stories of this kind, and was happy to cash in on it, ultimately compiling a rich catalogue of brief stories detailing all manner of exotic fetishisms and perversions, but his consequent reputation left something to be desired. He would never be regarded as a writer of the first rank in his own country, and there was no possibility of his being translated into English. The work of making male homosexuality acceptable as a literary theme was left for Proust and Gide to do.

In 1887 Lorrain left Montmartre to install himself in an apartment in the Rue de Courty, which he was able to furnish according to his own calculatedly bizarre taste. The phantasmagorical aspects of this private world were considerably exaggerated by the fact that he had begun drinking ether. His motive for doing this was undoubtedly medicinal, and he was initially impressed by the sudden surge of vitality which a dose of the drug gave him when he was ill or exhausted; it was one of the many "cures" with which he attempted to combat his increasing periods of debilitation. Under the hallucinogenic influence of ether, though, his apartments soon came to seem literally and figuratively haunted.

Those of Lorrain's short stories which do not deal with sexual perversity are mostly supernatural, and his works in this vein became increasingly strange and horrific, more akin to the works of E. T. A. Hoffmann than Poe. Much of his finest work is in this vein, and he wrote some very striking stories of bizarre apparitions and peculiar obsessions. He was later to write a self-conscious cycle of *"contes d'un buveur d'éther,"* which were included in *Sensations et souvenirs* (1895), but the effects of the drug can clearly be seen in the stories in his other collections, particularly *Buveurs d'âmes* (1893) and *Histoires de masques* (1900). Lorrain began to see the world itself as a great masque, and ether as means of unmasking the horrors which lurked behind all its false faces, hidden by masks and disguised by heavy makeup.

In 1888 Lorrain left the *Courrier* for *L'Événement*, where he was given a regular column in which to extend his mordant literary criticism into a more general critique of contemporary Parisian society. He called his essays along these lines "Pall-Malls," after the English weekly *The Pall Mall Gazette*, which had been edited since 1883 by W. T. Stead. Stead was an odd combination of muckraker and crusader, who became a role model for many later journalists; his exposés of the London brothels which specialized in flagellation and child prostitution caused a great sensation, which was magnified still further when he was condemned to a period of hard labor after buying a child from her mother in order to demonstrate how readily children were sold into prostitution.

Lorrain's image of the English gentry seems to have been largely formed by Stead's lurid articles, and he set out to do similar disservice to his own countrymen. His political stance was a curious kind of "right-wing anarchism" based in a scornful hatred of both capitalism and socialism. He was a nationalist through and through, despising the revolutionaries of 1789 for their bourgeois tendencies, but the fact that he became a diehard opponent of the Dreyfusards probably had far more to do with his long-standing dislike for Zola than any judgment of Dreyfus's culpability. (Lorrain was also outspokenly anti-Semitic, but that too might have been a byproduct of his personal detestation of Judith Gautier's Jewish ex-husband.) Problems with obtaining payment for his work led him to quit *L'Événement* in 1890 for the *Écho de Paris*, to which he was a prolific contributor—under various pseudonyms—until 1895, after which he worked mainly for *Le Journal*.

At the end of 1890 Lorrain left his haunted house in the Rue de Courty and moved to Auteuil. By this time his recurrent fevers were complicated by syphilis. Sarah Bernhardt, who did little else for him, at least referred him to a competent physician: the celebrated chirurgeon Dr. Pozzi, who was a colorful and well-known character in his own right. Pozzi instructed Lorrain to stop taking ether, advising him that his gut had become so badly ulcerated due to the effects of the drug that surgical intervention was necessary. Pozzi carried out the operation, removing a section of the small intestine, in 1893.

Despite his health problems Lorrain travelled to Spain and Algeria in 1892, the first of several expeditions abroad. He was joined in Auteuil by his mother, who lived with him until his death—a slightly mixed blessing, given her dogged disapproval of his lifestyle, but a blessing nevertheless. He was now earning good money and was able to support her in style; he sent her to the very best couturiers and had her painted by the noted portraitist Antonio de la Gandara (who also did the most striking portrait of Lorrain himself).

Lorrain formed several new friendships with women around this time. The first—and the one of which his mother most fervently disapproved, especially when rumors began to circulate about a possible marriage—was with the exotic Liane de Pougy, a performing artiste of sorts whose great ambition was to be the most fashionable and most expensive whore in Paris: a perfect *femme fatale*. Lorrain wrote "pantomimes" for her, just as he composed songs for the more respectable pianist Yvette Guilbert, whom he met the following year. Between 1892 and 1896 Lorrain was also frequently in the company of Jeanne Jacquemin, an artist in pastels, who shared his intense fascination with the occult. Together they explored the Underworld whose fashionability had been enhanced by *Là-bas*.

Jeanne Jacquemin's husband was a friend of Verlaine, and did not seem to mind the wayward lifestyle she adopted. She liked to pose as a notable figure in Decadent Paris—she claimed intimate acquaintance with Georges Rodenbach and Rémy de Gourmont—but she tended to be jealously possessive, and Lorrain fell out with her before setting off on his second trip to Algiers. He did not see her again for some years, and she faded out of the Paris scene; unfortunately, she neither forgot nor forgave him for his desertion.

****

In 1896 Lorrain was probably the best-paid journalist in Paris, and he had reached the summit of his brief celebrity. It is rather ironic that he is best remembered today for an incident which attracted little attention at the time, but which now figures as an episode in the many biographies of Marcel Proust. Lorrain twice attacked Proust's first book, *Les Plaisirs et les jours* (1896), the second time in an article published in January 1897. The slanders were no worse than Lorrain's customary stock-in-trade, but Proust sent his seconds to demand satisfaction, and the two men met on 6 February, armed with pistols. Two shots were discharged harmlessly, and the two men then shook hands.

Lorrain continued to make friends as well as enemies, particularly among the people he met in the home of Jean de Tinan, where Rachilde was a frequent fellow-guest. It was there that he made the acquaintance of Pierre Louÿs, whose lush erotic fantasy set in ancient Alexandria, *Aphrodite*, took Paris by storm in 1896. He also met the poet Henri de Régnier, the pioneering surrealist Alfred Jarry, and Colette, who seemed to like him far better than many of the women with whom he kept closer company. The circle dissipated when Tinan died, not long before Lorrain decided that he had to leave Paris for the sake of his health and removed his household to the balmier climes of Nice.

It is significant that Lorrain abandoned Paris at the end of 1900. For ten years he had been the self-appointed chronicler of the *fin de siècle*: the fascinated celebrant and sometime scourge of the folkways of Decadent Paris. A great deal of his rhetoric had drawn on the fact that the nineteenth century was winding down, approaching an end that was devoutly to be desired. He was very conscious of the extent to which that rhetoric would lose its force once the new century was born, and this consciousness was reinforced by the spectacular *Exposition Universelle* held in Paris in 1900.

Lorrain's career suddenly went into decline in 1900. It was as if he had fallen out of fashion instantly, by prior appointment. He continued to write for *Le Journal*, but he now gave priority to a new endeavor: the writing of two novels which would provide a kind of retrospective summary of the Decadent Movement and the world which had given birth to it. Huysmans had begun the movement with *A rebours* and Lorrain set out to provide it with a fitting conclusion. The two novels in question were *Monsieur de Phocas* (1901) and *Le Vice errant* (1902). They were were not greeted with any great popular acclaim.

Things began to go badly wrong for Lorrain immediately after these two novels appeared in print. Jeanne Jacquemin, seemingly repentant of her colorful past, recognized herself in Madame de Charmaille, one of the characters in a nouvelle called "Les Pelléastres," which was serialized in *Le Journal*. Lorrain had grafted attributes of his friends on to his fictional characters many times before—often unflatteringly, as in *Monsieur de Bougrelon* (1897), whose central character is a sharp caricature of Barbey d'Aurevilly—without any significant comeback, but Jeanne Jacquemin sued him for defamation of character. The case generated a great deal of bad publicity, and Lorrain was attacked from all sides by those who had once walked in fear of his sarcasm. The court—perhaps desirous of making an example of him, although it is unclear whose benefit the judges had in mind—required him to pay astonishingly high damages of 80,000 francs.

The settlement of this suit left Lorrain broke and vulnerable; he was soon to face a second lawsuit and—perhaps more seriously, in terms of his reputation—a formal charge of corrupting public morals by literary means, brought against *Monsieur de Phocas*. A similar charge had once been the making of Baudelaire's reputation, but in Lorrain's case the accusation only served to illustrate how dramatically the tide had turned, and how ardently the people of twentieth-century Paris desired to advertise that the nineteenth century was dead and gone. Lorrain was disappointed that hardly anyone came forward to speak in his defense (Colette was one exception), and particularly hurt by the fact that Huysmans remained silent.

Lorrain threw himself into his writing in order to pay the debts he had accrued. He continued to produce work at a furious pace, but much of it was pure hackwork. *La Maison Philibert* (1904), a calculatedly scabrous novel about a brothel, is of some interest as a Decadent work, but the other novels of this period were much weaker. His health continued to deteriorate, and his tuberculosis returned in full force in 1905. He took various "cures" in the spas of the Riviera, but they left him sicker than before. With typically grim irony he began signing his articles in *Le Journal* and *La Vie parisienne* "Le Cadavre."

In June 1906 Lorrain returned to Paris to help organize an art exhibition and to involve himself in an adaptation for the opera of one of his *contes*, *La Princess sous verre* (1896). He took the opportunity to consult Pozzi, who called in several colleagues to second his opinion that Lorrain's gut was so badly ulcerated that an operation could not help. Pozzi could only prescribe palliative measures, and it was in the course of following this prescription that Lorrain died. He was found unconscious in his bathroom, having perforated his colon while attempting to give himself an enema.

He died two days later, without having regained consciousness.

* * * * * * *

Lorrain was far from being the most accomplished writer involved in the Decadent Movement, but he was the one whose life and art were bound together into the most seamless whole. He was the man who embodied, more intimately and more inescapably than any other, the absurdities, affectations, paradoxes, and perversities of the Decadent style and the Decadent worldview. Baudelaire died without ever being fully conscious of what he had invented; Rimbaud gave up literary work as soon as he was old enough to know better; Verlaine came late to the celebration of Decadence and never could make up his mind whether he wanted to be a part of it or not; Huysmans graced the Movement with his brief presence and then went on about his private business; Rachilde wore a Decadent mask while retaining a secure hold on private respectability (and lived to the ripe old age of ninety-three!); Jean Lorrain, on the other hand, threw himself so completely into the Movement that it consumed his whole existence and condemned him to a horribly ignominious death.

Whereas *A rebours* had defined Decadent taste and the Decadent quest in advance of the Movement, Lorrain's *Monsieur de Phocas* provided an analysis after the fact. *A rebours* is, of course, a much finer work in literary terms, having the great advantages of originality and deftly vitriolic wit. *Monsieur de Phocas*, by its very nature, could have no such advantages; it looks back upon something already dead. It remains, however, a very interesting text and an invaluable key to the decadent consciousness.

Monsieur de Phocas is a much-extended and considerably rewritten version of the title-story of Lorrain's collection *Un Démoniaque* (1895). The substance of several other short stories is recruited to the task of fleshing it out; it thus represents a recapitulation and reformulation of work originally done in a more flamboyant spirit. It is possible that Lorrain's motive for re-working the material was purely commercial, but what he accomplished was a summary collation of ideas about the quality of life in *fin de siècle* Paris—the metropolis which a posthumous collection of his articles was to dub *la ville empoisonnée*: the Poisoned City. The manuscript left behind by the eponymous anti-hero of the novel when he sets off for the mysterious East is effectively a catalogue of all the Poisoned City's horrors and ignominies. It is also a testament to the darkly seductive magnetism of its suburban low-life, as experienced by a nobly-born, fabulously rich, contemptuously aloof, and direly neurasthenic character: a character who is in some strange sense the specter (or "larva") which Jean Lorrain occasionally glimpsed when he looked at himself in a mirror, lurking behind the painted and powdered mask which was his face.

Like *A rebours*, *Monsieur de Phocas* is cast as a first-person account of the adventures of a nobleman who supposedly embodies the malaise of an epoch: an epoch whose reality repels him while certain aspects of its art entrance him. The central characters of the two novels, however—which must be regarded as fantastic extrapolations of their authors' contrasting personalities—could hardly have been more different.

Jean Des Esseintes is eccentric and neurasthenic, but he is also very methodical; his opposition to the values of the world from which he is trying to isolate himself may be exaggerated to the point of grotesquerie, but it is closely reasoned and it is underpinned by an articulate and ingenious philosophy. He has a definite blueprint for the ideal existence, which he sets out to actualize with the utmost care in the privacy of his own home. Whatever his failings, he never doubts that the solution to his problems lies within himself, and he strives with all his might to be a paragon of self-sufficiency.

The Duc de Fréneuse, who eventually renames himself Monsieur de Phocas, is not at all methodical, nor has he any plan to which method might be applied. He has a problem, in which impuissance, ennui, spleen, and neurasthenic sickness all play their various parts, but he has no idea where to look for a solution. Instead of remaining at home he must go out into the world, conducting a frenzied search without even knowing what he is looking for, following the lure of an elusive and illusory blue-green glint which he occasionally sees in the eyes of certain works of art (primarily and most particularly in those of a bust of Antinoüs, the handsome youth whose drowning caused such grief to the emperor Hadrian).

Far from being a paragon of self-sufficiency, Fréneuse is desperate to find a guide: someone who can take him in hand and guide him to peace of mind. He briefly hopes that the dancer Izé Kranile might somehow save him from himself, but her stage presence turns out to be a mere illusion; in the flesh she is horribly coarse. He is beset by dreams and hallucinations, most of which feature masks. He begins to see his fellow human beings as cadavers and monsters wearing masks of flesh, and it is while he is in the grip of one such fit that he encounters Claudius Ethal, an English painter who seems to understand what he is seeing and promises to cure him.

Fréneuse's attitude to Ethal is a hectic confusion of opposites; he is fascinated by him and hopeful that he can effect the promised cure, but he is also terrified by him and fearful that the association will lead him to damnation. Ethal instructs Fréneuse to study various works of art, most of them monstrous: Jan Toorop's *The Three Brides*, etchings by Goya and James Ensor, an ancient and decaying wax doll, and his own waxen image of a dying boy. Ethal also invites him to a *soirée* where he encounters a series of social grotesques embodying every aspect of the Decadent lifestyle, at which a powerful hallucinogenic drug dispatches the Duc on an extended dream-odyssey in which visions of India are the prelude to a nightmare of vampiric predation.

Fréneuse is taken home from this *soirée* by Ethal's mournful friend Thomas Welcome, who warns him not to fall under Ethal's spell, and insists that his own life has been spoiled by Ethal's influence. Welcome intends to return to the East, and urges the Duc to go with him, insisting that it is the only possible route of escape from his ills—but Ethal offers a more cynical account of Welcome's character and motives.

Fréneuse tries to find other escape-routes, returning briefly to his family estate in Normandy in the hope that he might there recover the innocence of his childhood, but it is hopeless. He returns to Paris to take in two more exhibitions of art. The first is a visit to Gustave Moreau's studio, to study his many images of *femmes fatales* and to make a detailed examination of "Les Prétendants." The second is a visit to Ethal's apartment, to view three portraits of beautiful women which constitute the artist's finest achievement.

The Duc's appreciation of these portraits is utterly spoiled by Ethal's commentary on the moral failings of the ladies involved, which drives home the insidious message that their beauty, as captured by the undeniable genius of the artist, is a mere mask. This relentless subversion (or corruption, as Fréneuse prefers to designate it) drives the Duc to the extreme of forcing Ethal to drink the poison contained in a huge ring—the "Eye of Eboli"—which he delights in wearing.

Having committed this murder, Fréneuse is possessed by a wonderful sense of freedom; he renames himself Monsieur de Phocas, and after experiencing one last dream-vision of the blue-green eyes— this time in association with Astarté—he sets off joyfully to join Thomas Welcome in Benares.

* * * * * *

The differences between *A rebours* and *Monsieur de Phocas* are clearly reflected in the lives of their two authors. It seems that Huysmans really did think that some solution to his own existential predicament might be found if he could only figure it out, and that the solution was to be found in a readjustment of his own attitude of mind. Lorrain never had that kind of self-confidence, and everything that happened to him intensified his awareness of its lack. He recognized early in life that he was never going to be accepted by the social élite, and he was inexorably drawn to the bitter conclusion that his sexual inclinations—which were not merely homosexual but ran very definitely to what would now be called "rough trade"—were as absurd as they were irresistible.

If ever a man were damned, it was Jean Lorrain, and the fact that contemporary Paris could hold up a mirror in which he could readily perceive the relative success of others slightly more blessed undoubtedly increased his chagrin. It is not surprising that the darkest of all his fabular *contes*—which became increasingly dark as his career advanced—is "Narkiss" (1898), a bizarrely transfigured and inverted version of the myth of Narcissus. Nor is it surprising that his archetypal image of the Decadent personality should be a man fatally and irredeemably obsessed by a mirage.

Given that he was not only narcissistic but proud, it is understandable that in his darker moods Lorrain would flirt with self-hatred, and with the notion—both direly horrible and perversely comforting—that he might be mad. He knew full well, of course, that *A rebours* was a black comedy; although it contains fewer jokes, *Monsieur de Phocas* is also a comedy of sorts. The novel's grotesquerie is calculated and its irony cuts much deeper than may initially be apparent. The conclusion at which the Duc de Fréneuse ultimately arrives is, of course, no redemption at all; it is best regarded as the blackly ironic climax of a *conte cruel*—and its irony is very black indeed.

The contending forces surrounding the Duc, pulling him forcibly in different directions with scant regard for the authority of his own vacillating will, are incarnated within the story as actual persons (or, at least, as the images of persons). The most powerful and the most problematic among these forces is the odious Ethal; if we are to understand the novel and its author we must first understand Ethal.

Some commentators have suggested that Ethal is based on Oscar Wilde. This identification is undoubtedly encouraged by the fact that Ethal arrives in Paris, having exiled himself to Paris in the wake of a lawsuit involving one "Lord Kerneby," but it would probably be a mistake to take it too seriously. Lorrain was an admirer of Wilde, and used one of his "Pall-Malls" to launch a searing attack on the English hypocrisy which had condemned Wilde to hard labor and wrecked his career; he met Wilde in the early 1890s, when his friend Marcel Schwob—also a writer of supernatural vignettes and wryly dark *contes*—brought Wilde to dine at his house, and Lorrain thought that occasion sufficiently auspicious to invite Anatole France as well. There is no reason to suppose that Lorrain's attitude to the English writer was such as to license the kind of parody that would have been involved in transforming him into Ethal. We need not accept the Duc de Fréneuse's view that Ethal is an archetype of evil—his own account of himself is more convincing than the Duc's paranoid and rumor-based fantasies—in order to recognize that if Ethal were based on any real person the characterization would be horribly unflattering.

The text itself gives us a different account of the manner in which the character of Ethal might have been inspired. He is explicitly linked to a painting by Antonio Moro of a dwarf kept as a jester by the

Duc D'Albe (and he does indeed function as a kind of jester, whose malicious buffoonery masks an all-too-perceptive wisdom). Ethal's rival within the plot, Thomas Welcome—who has a very different notion of how the Duc's existential malaise can be cured—is likewise associated with a painting, but this time a purely hypothetical image produced by Ethal himself. Welcome thus becomes a kind of "secondary creation": the more appealing aspect of the equivocally threatening Ethal. The text is always telling us how inextricably bound together they are, licensing the view that they are two parts of the same whole.

****

The most useful key to the decoding of these symbols is undoubtedly the names attached to the characters. Lorrain rarely gave his characters realistic names and was fond of calculatedly awkward wordplay. To an English reader there is nothing in the least abstruse about "Welcome," but French readers would probably have found the other two names more obvious in their implication. "Fréneuse" is an adjectival modification of *frénésie* (the actual adjective is *frénétique*), straightforwardly translatable as "frenzied." "Ethal" is superficially reminiscent of *étal* (a butcher's meat-stall; *étalage* refers more generally to window-dressing and vulgar ostentation), but if that name too is regarded as a deliberately-botched adjective, then the noun from which it comes is surely *éther*.

Ethal's role in the plot—he is a "thought-reader" who gets inside the Duc's head and feeds his fantasies, all the while pretending to be working towards a cure for all his ills—can certainly be regarded as a phantasmagorical extrapolation of the role played in Lorrain's life by ether. If we elect to interpret things according to this pattern, then Thomas Welcome's alternative cure, although studiously couched in terms of the familiar Decadent rhetoric regarding the virtues of culture unspoiled by civilization, becomes suspiciously akin to the kind of cure by benign climate which was the nineteenth century's most hopeful treatment for tuberculosis. The fact that Welcome's travel brochure—according to Ethal, at least—deceptively neglects the forces of "base prostitution" may be taken to reflect the awareness (which no Decadent was without) that the sun can do nothing at all for syphilis. It is no coincidence that the figurine of Astarté which features in the plot has a death's-head superimposed on her genitals, nor that Fréneuse suspects at one point that the "mouth of shadow" whispering ideas of murder in his ear might be the voice of this death's-head.

Seen in this light, the Duc de Fréneuse's struggle is entirely internal. Given that we are conscientiously reminded that his account has gaping logical flaws—the dating of the last few entries is nonsensical—we may be entitled to wonder whether Claudius Ethal has any existence outside the feverish brain of the Duc de Fréneuse. Perhaps he is a mere hallucination conjured up by stress: the externalization of an enemy within. If so, the "murder" is merely one more fantastic vision, one more desperate gyration in the Duc's frenzied but hopeless quest to find someone or something to turn to.

There is, of course, one name in the text which has no function except to be symbolic: Monsieur de Phocas. Lorrain would have been familiar with that name in two contexts. Saint Phocas, the patron saint of gardeners, was a popular subject of contemporary poems and essays; he had recently been featured in *Phocas le jardinier* (1898) by the American-born poet Francis Viélé-Griffin. There was also a Byzantine emperor named Phocas (whose name is nowadays usually rendered Phokas). Monsieur de Phocas does seem to be claiming descent from the latter's distinguished family, but it is probable that the real significance of his name is a phonetic play on words. The Duc de Fréneuse changes his name because he thinks that he has finally got his life, and his predicament, "in focus" (focus itself was not commonly used in French at the turn of the century, but the adjectives *focal* and *focaux* were fairly familiar in technical discourse).

It is, of course, obvious to the sensitive reader that whether Monsieur de Phocas joins Thomas Welcome in Benares or not, he has no hope whatsoever of making any kind of satisfactory contact with the magical gaze which fascinates him. The text informs us that he has indeed brought his vision of Astarté into focus, but the fact that her genital region is carefully screened from view ensures that she remains as elusive as ever. No matter how wonderfully exotic Benares may be (and it certainly seems so in Thomas Welcome's lyrical description), it is of this world and not out of it; it cannot answer the plea of the Decadent poet's soul. Whatever "fervor" the virile races of the un-Decadent East might possess, and whatever effect that fervor might have on the way they live, it is not something that can heal the existential wounds of the Duc de Fréneuse, nor even those of his alter ego Monsieur de Phocas. Ethal or no Ethal, Welcome or no Welcome, the author of the tale which is told in Lorrain's novel is well and truly damned.

All the honest Decadents knew—at least by the time they found out what had actually happened to Arthur Rimbaud when he put an end to his *saison en enfer* by going to the East and hurling himself into a very different way of life—that there was no way out of their particular blind alley. There was no escape from the Poisoned City, once its poison had been absorbed; Jean Lorrain knew and accepted that. In the end, as Jean Des Esseintes had proposed, the only consolation which could hold at bay the ravages of spleen, syphilis, and all their kindred ills was to be found in works of art, and in the comforts and petty luxuries of modern artifice. The underlying horrors of life could not in the end be defeated; they could only be disguised by masks, paints, and powders. Such refuges could not possibly constitute a cure, but they did provide a valuable and welcome series of palliative measures.

Unfortunately, as Jean Lorrain found out when he blew a gaping hole in his ulcerated colon, some kinds of corruption inflict wounds to which palliative measures can offer no relief.

VII.

ANGELS OF PERVERSITY:

RÉMY DE GOURMONT'S
RETREAT FROM THE WORLD

Nobody ever really tried to follow Jean Des Esseintes's example, retiring from the Decadent world to a private palace selectively furnished with the best consolatory comforts that money could buy. It was not so much the lack of Des Esseintes's means that inhibited them—although that would, of course, have made matters difficult—as the lack of his awesome psychological self-sufficiency. No matter how much they affected to despise the world as a whole, the Decadents remained essentially gregarious; they valued friendship and good conversation, and they were as keenly interested as any other writers in the critical reception of their work.

Such is the irony of fate, however, that one of the principal figures of the Decadent Movement was eventually forced into a kind of exile, which gave him no alternative but to cultivate a special kind of privacy and to maintain his social contacts primarily by means of the written word. His life story is as interesting, in its own way—and as ironically instructive—as Jean Lorrain's.

Rémy de Gourmont was born in 1858, the scion of an aristocratic family which had suffered a drastic decline in its fortunes, mainly due to the depredations of the English during the Napoléonic wars. When he was ten years old the family was forced to leave the Château de la Motte at Bazoches-en-Houlmes, where he had been born, and take up residence in the somewhat less grandiose Manoir de Mesnil-Villeman not far from Coutances, where he went to school. In 1876 he went to Caen to study law, but he was no more inclined to accept the law as a vocation than Jean Lorrain.

In 1877 Gourmont's parents gave him leave to continue his studies in Paris. He knew before leaving for the capital that he would soon abandon all pretence of preparation for the legal profession. He confided to his personal diary his intention to devote himself to "*l'amour et les livres*," scrupulously noting that love would enable him to develop the sensual aspect of his personality, and books the intellectual aspect. He was to remain permanently preoccupied with notions of personal evolution and self-development, and with the supposed divisions, balances, tensions, and contradictions inherent in the idea of the self. He was perpetually fascinated by dichotomies of all kinds: male and female; thought and emotion; materialism and idealism; God and man.

Gourmont's intellectual exploration of the dynamics of such complementarities and oppositions drew him into all manner of heresies, but no matter what challenges he posed to the religious and aristocratic ideals which he had inherited, he never entirely cast them aside. As with Baudelaire and Huysmans, Gourmont's flirtations with atheism and literary Satanism remained firmly set within a Catholic context, and however radical his moral philosophy became, he was never in the least attracted by socialist politics; he remained a diehard elitist utterly contemptuous of "the rabble."

In 1881 Gourmont applied for a post in the Bibliothèque Nationale, although the stipend was scarcely sufficient to meet his living expenses. His early work included the preparation of a series of educational books for young readers. He also began publishing articles in periodicals, including *Le Monde* and *La Vie parisienne*. His first novel, *Merlette* (1886), is generally considered to be awkward and naive; the manuscript of a second, *Patrice*, was lost by the journal to which it was submitted—a loss which he does not seem to have regretted for very long. Whether his early adventures in love were as dubiously satisfactory as these early literary endeavors it is hard to tell, although he was a handsome young man before he fell prey to the disfiguring disease which drove him into seclusion.

Gourmont's romantic aspirations took a decisive new turn in 1887, when he met Berthe Courrière. She was six years his senior, and her aristocratic pretensions—she preferred to style herself Berthe de Courrière—were so obviously specious that even Rachilde, who was no stranger to the business of fantastic self-aggrandizement, felt free to describe her as a "horribly bourgeois fantasist"; nevertheless, she captivated Gourmont. His early letters to her were posthumously published as *Lettres à Sixtine*, clearly associating her with the heroine of his first successful novel *Sixtine* (1890), and there is no doubt that *Le Fantôme* (1891) is an account of their affair, albeit highly transfigured by jaundiced hindsight. The female protagonist of *Le Fantôme* is named Hyacinthe, and it was not by coincidence that this was also the forename of Madame Chantelouve in *Là-bas*; Berthe Courrière was, of course, Huysmans's principal guide to the occult Underworld of Paris.

Berthe Courrière widened Gourmont's horizons considerably, in both erotic and social terms. She introduced him to Huysmans, and for a while the two men became fast friends, although the friendship eventually weakened for much the same reasons that Huysmans' association with Jean Lorrain became more distant. Like Huysmans, Gourmont became a great admirer and early critical champion of the poetry and prose-poetry of Mallarmé, and Huysmans presumably encouraged Gourmont's decision to develop Symbolist techniques of his own with a fervor which would exceed even Mallarmé's.

* * * * * * *

Gourmont formed other equally important friendships at this time, one of the most significant being with Villiers de L'Isle-Adam, with whom he had a good deal in common. Like Gourmont, Villiers was an aristocrat whose family had fallen on hard times, and who felt it very keenly. The failure of Villiers's attempts to marry for money had embittered him against the world and against the female sex in particular. Although Gourmont did not share the older man's mordant worldview at first, he was soon to drink as deeply from his own cup of bitterness.

The sub-genre of *contes cruels* to which Villiers had given a name in his collection of 1883 paraded a kind of haughty cynicism which Gourmont found attractive, and which infected his own work to a considerable degree. It is clearly manifest in the cynical erotic fantasies which he collected under the title *Histoires magiques* (1894). Alas, this friendship did not even last as long as Gourmont's association with Huysmans; it was cut short in 1889 when Villiers died.

Gourmont also became friendly with Alfred Vallette, the husband of the amazing Rachilde. This association proved far more durable; Gourmont assisted Vallette in assuming the proprietorship of the *Mercure de France* in 1890, and became one of its most prolific contributors. It was for this journal that Gourmont was to do much of the work which first made his reputation, although the respect which he eventually earned was initially preceded by notoriety, occasioned by a contemptuous article for the *Mercure* on "Le Joujou-Patriotisme." This sarcastic attack on the dishonesty of ostentatious patriotism so offended the political establishment that Gourmont was dismissed from his post at the Bibliothèque Nationale. The ensuing scandal provoked contributions from Catulle Mendès and Octave Mirbeau, among others, although the anarchist Mirbeau—whose support Gourmont presumably regarded as a mixed blessing—had difficulty finding a publisher for his own even more outspoken comments.

Later, Gourmont was to make a friend of the young Alfred Jarry, whom he met in the offices of the *Mercure de France* in 1894. He collaborated with Jarry on *L'Ymagier* (1896), and exerted a significant influence on the development of the younger writer, but as with Huysmans the association was eventually split by an irreconcilable difference of opinion.

Although his first publication—the text for an illustrated educational book on the eruption of a volcano—had been issued in 1882 and he had been a reasonably prolific writer ever since, the work which Gourmont did in the period 1889-91 marked a new beginning. It was in this period that he wholeheartedly embraced Symbolist techniques and cultivated a thoroughly Decadent sensibility, although he had his reservations about the applicability of the term "Decadence." His fiction of the period consisted mainly of brief *contes*, and there is a considerable grey area where these overlap with his experiments in prose-poetry. His one and only subject matter was sex; he was deeply fascinated by the essential capriciousness of the sexual impulse, by the ill-effects of social and religious repression of sexuality, and by the intellectual strategies which might maximize the quasi-transcendental experience of sexual rapture.

The stories collected in *Histoires magiques*, which appeared in various journals in 1890-91, display a good deal of creative exuberance and sheer literary virtuosity. They feature extravagant play with the new-found techniques of symbolism: the symbolism of colors, of flowers, and of religious imagery is elaborately explored and developed. The proliferation of sexual symbolism in these works is quite extraordinary, echoing in advance much of the mapping that Freud was soon to do in *The Interpretation of Dreams*. In Gourmont's *Les Histoires magiques*, as in Freudian dreams, everything is symbolic in some sexual sense—but in Gourmont's tales, wish-fulfillment is at best only half the story, almost always being followed by disillusionment.

In the most deliciously delicate of these tales, "Danaette," the eponymous protagonist surrenders, body and soul, to the spirit of a snowstorm which whisks her away to a fabulous realm where "all the dear little adulteresses, eternally beloved, were endlessly enraptured by the impatient and imperious caresses of the angels of perversity." In the most strikingly horrific of them, "Péhor," the innocent Douceline's fondness for masturbation render her vulnerable to the attentions of the eponymous demon, who destroys her horribly when her first adventure in sexual intercourse infects her with syphilis. In the most earnestly subtle of them, "La Robe blanche," a young man is deeply disappointed by the discovery that the dictates of divine love cannot compete with the vulgar ordinances of society.

From the very beginning, Gourmont was well aware of the mercuriality of sexual fulfillment, and the extreme difficulty of making the most of it. The magnitude of his disappointment was, however, unusual. In the slightly more substantial works which concluded this phase of his career, "Stratagems" (the novelette which concludes *Les Histoires magiques*) and *Le Fantôme*, one can easily see the after effects of a decayed infatuation, but one can also see something more profound. It is highly probable that by the time they were written Gourmont was aware of the first symptoms of the disease which wrecked his life, and was suffering altogether reasonably premonitions of permanent loss.

****

The disease which began to cast its blight upon Gourmont's features in 1891 was known at the time as "tubercular lupus." As that name implies, it was widely—but incorrectly—assumed to be a species of tuberculosis. It is nowadays known as "discoid lupus erythematosus," and is generally thought to be caused by a virus, but even the modern pharmacopoeia has little to offer by way of effective treatment. The disease is not fatal, nor even particularly debilitating in cases in which it does not develop into the far more serious systemic lupus erythematosus, which affects the other organs of the body.

The progress of Gourmont's case was limited but rapid. Initially, it only affected his face, but to such an extent that it rapidly became the dominating fact of his life. His friends continued to visit him, but as time went by he became extremely reluctant to go out into a world where he was likely to be refused service in restaurants. He became a recluse, and went into hiding even within his own quarters. He made no very determined attempt to furnish these quarters in unduly plush style, because he was not so devoted to visual sumptuousness as Jean Des Esseintes or Jean Lorrain, but he took full advantage of the one reliable pathway that could lead him "anywhere out of the world": he became the most assiduous reader of his era, the great chronicler, critic, and philosophical analyst of the literature of his own and previous generations. His most important researches were collected in two revealingly-titled books: *Le Livre des masques* (1896) and *Le Chemin de velours* (1902), translated, respectively, as *The Book of Masks* and *The Velvet Path*.

Arthur Ransome appended to his translation of Gourmont's novel, *A Night in the Luxembourg*, a brief memoir of the author, whom he visited in his hideaway. Ransome found Gourmont—who was then nearing the premature end of his life—living on the fourth floor of a house in the Rue de Saints-Pères, dressed in a monk's robe and a grey felt cap. He records that Gourmont was careful to place his visitors on the far side of his huge desk, with the lamplight carefully directed towards their faces, allowing his own to remain steeped in shadow. He also observes that Gourmont kept his hand continually in front of his face during their conversation. He does not, however, take the trouble to explain why Gourmont did these things—and most biographical sketches of Gourmont in English reference books carefully make no mention of his disease, although no French reference book considers it unmentionable. One can only wonder what readers unaware of the truth of the matter might have made of Ransome's circumlocutory observation that the face which was once "beautiful in the youth of the flesh" had now become "beautiful in the age of the mind....vitalized by intellectual activity."

Having lost his position at the Bibliothèque Nationale, Gourmont had already begun to make his living entirely with his pen. His forced retirement from the world made it possible for him to concentrate his energies to this end in a very methodical manner. In the course of the following quarter-century he produced enough work to fill fifty volumes, most of it taking the initial form of essays written for periodicals.

Gourmont's scholarly work covered a wide range, from his early study of mysticism and symbolism in Medieval poetry, *Le Latin mystique* (1892) to his remarkable study of the natural history of sexuality, *Physique de l'amour, essai sur l'instinct sexuel* (1903), which was translated by Ezra Pound as *The Natural Philosophy of Love* in 1922. His studies in "the culture of ideas" helped to interpret and popularize the philosophical ideas of Schopenhauer and Nietzsche, and he made considerable contributions of his own to the development of aesthetic philosophy. Not all his non-fiction was scholarly, though; his reclusiveness did not prevent him from being a prolific letter-writer, and some of his later works take the form of quirky epistles, including the satirical *Lettres d'un satyre* (1913) and the (authentic) *Lettres à l'Amazone* (1914) whose addressee was Natalie Barney, one of several notable "amazons" who applied to the prefecture of police for a license to wear male attire in public (others included George Sand and Rachilde). The latter book was published the year before Gourmont died, serving as a suitably eccentric swan song.

Gourmont wrote four more novels during the period of his voluntary incarceration: *Les Chevaux de Diomède* (1897); *Le Songe d'une femme* (1899); *Une Nuit au Luxembourg* (1906); and *Un Coeur virginal* (1907). With the partial exception of *Une Nuit au Luxembourg*, however, these reflective and rather distant works are very different from the conscientiously Decadent works of his early Symbolist period, whose climactic phase came to an end with the fervent heretical drama *Lilith* (1892), and the various short stories and prose-poems which were collected in *Proses moroses* (1894), *Le Pèlerin du silence* (1896), and *D'un pays lointain* (1898).

Some of the work in these collections dates from the 1889-91 period, notably "Le Pèlerin du silence," a nouvelle dedicated to Mallarmé which appeared in the *Mercure de France* in 1890, but the later stories collected in *D'un pays lointain* have a much blacker edge than the *Histoires magiques*: the "faraway land" is the barbaric past, but his imaginary journeys there are no ordinary adventures in escapism, and they contrast sharply with such overripe Romantic fantasies as Gautier's. They are vividly baroque, but also deeply uncomfortable, and it is not surprising that Gourmont eventually gave up writing them—nor that when he returned to escapist fantasy in *Une Nuit au Luxembourg* he did so in a fervently nostalgic vein. In the latter part of his career he produced only one more volume of short pieces, *Couleurs* (1908). This was titled for a set of effete exercises in color-symbolism, but the volume had to be padded out with material reprinted from *Proses moroses*.

****

Gourmont's thoughts on the idea of Decadence were set out at some length in an essay on "Stéphane Mallarmé and the Idea of Decadence" (1898), which was written immediately after Mallarmé's death and reprinted in *La Culture des idées* (1900). Here Gourmont follows an argumentative line very different from that of his rival theorist Paul Bourget, and carefully casts doubt on the kind of biological analogies which had long been bandied about by believers in hereditary degeneracy and neurasthenia.

The headquote of the essay is taken from from one of Baudelaire's letters, which describes the term Decadence as "a very convenient word for ignorant pedagogues; a vague word behind which our laziness and lack of curiosity concerning the law seek shelter." Gourmont is scathing about the analogy which had so often been drawn between the fates of empires and individuals, describing Montesquieu's ideas as "puerile," and observing that far more empires have died violently at the height of their powers than have crumbled away as if diseased.

What literary historians usually mean by a period of "decadence," Gourmont argues, is simply the absence of notable writers and the consequent prevalence of imitation. He goes on to say, however, that the idea of Decadence which is associated with Mallarmé has undergone a dramatic *bouleversement*, being assimilated with what was formerly its opposite: the idea of innovation. This has come about, he says, because the world of Academe has become suspicious of all art which is not imitative, and has sought to stigmatize innovation by decrying its "decadence."

In spite of all this, when Gourmont finally goes on to analyze the precious quality of Mallarmé's work, he still does so in terms of a biological analogy; significantly and typically, however, he reverses the implication usually taken from it. "When the brain is rich in sensations and in ideas," he says, "there is a constant eddy, and the smooth surface is troubled at the moment of spouting. Let us....prefer marshes swarming with life to a glass of clear water."

When he concludes Mallarmé's eulogy Gourmont does so with the words:

> it may well be that a poetry full of doubts, of shifting shades, and of ambiguous perfumes, can alone please us henceforward; and, if the word decadence really summed up all these autumnal, twilight charms, we might welcome it, even making it one of the keys of

the viol; but it is dead; the master is dead, the penultimate is dead.[1]

One can sympathize with the sadness which occasioned this judgment—all the more so when one recalls that a disease from which no other Decadent suffered had condemned Gourmont not merely to twilight but to virtual darkness—but it was premature. In 1898 decadence was not yet dead, but only decaying towards a twilight which was rather more prolonged than Gourmont could have anticipated. The marsh swarming with life might have become stagnant, but it was never to become sterile; anyone who drank from its turbid waters remained highly likely to suffer a certain systematic disturbance—temporary or permanent—in consequence.

Gourmont's use of biological analogies in this essay is entirely in keeping with his work as a whole. He was always interested in the biological roots of behavior, and the moral lessons which might be drawn from such knowledge. He was always dismissive of the analyses of men like Nordau, who had tried to tie literary accomplishments of which he approved to such unworthy notions as "degeneracy," and he was enthusiastic to offer a more satisfactory scheme of understanding. The scheme he chose to develop was, of course, based in the psychology of sex, which had always been the dominant subject of all his fiction. His typically Decadent interest in perversity displayed in *Histoires magiques* and *Le Fantôme* was gradually transformed into a theory of sexuality which was highly idiosyncratic and quite unprecedented.

Gourmont can easily be seen as a direct literary descendant of Théophile Gautier, much of whose fiction consists of erotic fantasies which lament the failure of actual sexual relationships to live up to the ideals of the imagination. As has previously been noted, though, Gautier achieved a compromise in life which is reflected in the self-indulgence of much of his fiction; while elevating the ballerina Carlotta Grisi to the status of a Platonic ideal he served his sexual appetite by sleeping with her sister Ernesta. Gourmont is much less sentimental and much more relentlessly analytical than Gautier; even in his earliest works he is never content to let his characters linger long in their fantasy-worlds. His sceptical intelligence rips such delusions to shreds almost as soon as they are formulated, and he is perpetually entranced by the apparent absurdity of sexual attraction.

The seeming impossibility of actually achieving a satisfactory sexual relationship undoubtedly disappointed Gautier, but Gautier was prepared to make the best of what he had, both materially and imaginatively. For Gourmont that impossibility—once he had convinced himself of it—was a more profound tragedy, an expression of the essential perversity of existence. That perversity became a topic of intense interest to him, to be investigated and described and explained as fully as possible. His social isolation undoubtedly intensified this research, but it had already begun when the first symptoms of his disease became apparent.

The *Histoires magiques* are really neither "tales" nor "magical"; they are a series of case studies in sexual attraction, mapping the capricious forms which erotic attraction may take, and the sometime bizarre behaviors which result from its channelling. Where they become explicitly supernatural they do so purely by symbolic extension, although the sexual impulse itself is here represented as a quasi-supernatural force. It was the Catholic Church's attitude to sexuality, more than any purely doctrinal objection, which drove Gourmont to embrace attitudes so heretical that some people would indeed consider their literary expressions blasphemous. He was completely at odds with the Church's repression of sexuality, considering the social and psychological consequences of that repression to be appalling.

"Péhor," the story which Gourmont selected to open the sequence of his *Histoires magiques*, is a straightforward account of a young girl brought to destruction by her own sexuality, perverted by enforced ignorance and social pressure into a species of pious idolatry which cannot begin to satisfy her inner need. The eponymous demon was, of course, a tribal god before he was condemned as fallacious by the followers of Jehovah, when his status was automatically redefined as evil. The venereal disease which kills poor Douceline so brutally is something which shelters beneath the cloak of secrecy which the church has spread over the entire spectrum of sexual impulse and expression— and that is the true horror of the tale.

Before his disillusionment became complete, Gourmont was sufficiently inspired by the possibilities of sexual experience to endeavor to rework theology and ritual so as to produce a more honest and more life-enhancing species of Christianity. The primary result of this endeavor is a bizarre transfiguration of the Mass, whose imaginary ritual is described at some length in *Le Fantôme*—but Gourmont soon realized that such a superficial metamorphosis could not work. In order to redeem the perverse demons of sexuality one must do more than simply redefine them as angels, for the retention at the core of a re-sexualized religion of all those martyred saints and the crucified Christ inevitably places a kind of sado-masochism at the presumed heart of sexual experience—a move which the protagonist of *Le Fantôme* ultimately finds self-defeating. Other strategies outlined in the various *histoires magiques* are similarly revealed as direly destructive or ultimately self-contradictory.

* * * * * * *

Later in his career, Gourmont laid aside the elaborate metaphorical coat-of-many-colors which decorated—but also confined—his early short stories. He largely abandoned the intricate network of symbolic references in favor of a very different ideative context. He was aided in making this move by his reading of Nietzsche, whose attacks on the life-denying aspects of Christianity were even fiercer than his own, and whose interest in venturing "beyond good and evil" to a new and better morality he shared. Gourmont combined this influence with inspirations obtained from his reading of the works of the celebrated entomologist J. H. Fabre and other contemporary treatises on natural history and evolution. He drew upon observations made by Fabre and others to construct a "physiology of sex" which attempted to replace (and to some extent reposition) human sexuality within the context of a universal, multi-faceted, and intrinsically eccentric biological phenomenon.

Given the astonishing range of sexual behaviors to be found in the animal kingdom, especially among the invertebrates, the whimsicality of the human sexual impulse came to Gourmont to seem entirely expectable. In *Physique de l'amour* and many other essays he extensively elaborates an argument briefly cited (credited to Schopenhauer) in *Le Fantôme*, to the effect that there is no fundamental difference between intelligence and instinct, and that the phenomena of the human mind cannot and should not be attributed to the workings of some divinely-created soul which merely uses the body as a habitation. In this view, the variety of human sexual behavior becomes a phenomenon of nature to which moral commandments are essentially irrelevant:

> There are species in which the position of the organs is such that the same individual cannot be at the same time the female of the one for whom he is the male, but he can at that moment when he acts as male, serve as female to another male, who is female to a third, and so on. This explains the chaplets of spintrian gasteropods which one sees realizing, innocently and according to the ineluctable law of nature, carnal imaginings of which erotic humanity boasts. Viewed in the light of animal customs, debauchery loses all its character and lure, because it loses all claim to immorality. Man, who united in himself all the aptitudes of the animals, all their laborious instincts, all their industries, could not escape the heritage of their sexual methods: and there is no lewdness which has no normal type in nature.[2]

The literary extension of this philosophy is seen in *Une Coeur virginal*, which carries a preface explaining that it ought to be deemed a "physiological novel." It is, in essence, an elaborate account of how mate-choice in humans ought to transcend the customary romantic illusions, allowing itself to be dictated instead by the complementarity of physical needs—a complementarity which is much better reflected in the patterns of conventional immorality than in the sentimental mythology of "falling in love." This attitude—which leads in Gourmont's case to a disappointment as bitter as that expressed in the *conte cruel* aspects of the *Histoires magiques*—is manifest in the reflections of several of the characters in *Un Coeur virginal*, in such passages as this:

> He had often pondered on the mystery of intelligence among children. How is it that these subtle creatures are so quickly transformed into imbeciles? Why should the flower of these fine graceful plants be silliness?
>
> But isn't it the same with animals, and especially among the animals that approach our physiology most closely? The great apes, so intelligent in their youth, become idiotic and cruel as soon as they reach puberty. There is a cape there which they never double. A few men succeed; their intelligence escapes shipwreck, and they float free and smiling on the tranquilized sea. Sex is an absinthe whose strength only the strong can stand; it poisons the blood of the commonalty of men. Women succumb even more surely to this crisis.[3]

The extrapolation of these ideas provides a series of excuses for Gourmont's peculiar species of carefully-modified and sentimentally-mollified misogyny, whose beginnings—which might owe as much to the influence of Villiers de L'Isle-Adam as to the disenchanted aftermath of his affair with Berthe Courrière—can be seen in *Le Fantôme*. "Women are ruminants," the protagonist of *Un Coeur virginal* opines, not knowing quite whether he means it as an insult or a compliment; "they can live for months, for years it may be, on a voluptuous memory. That is what explains the apparent virtue of certain women; one lovely sin, like a beautiful flower with an immortal perfume, is enough to bless the days of their life."

The ideas of this phase in Gourmont's career were a significant influence on the theories of another well-known (but somewhat less careful) misogynist, Ezra Pound, who had assisted in the translation of the earlier novel *Les Chevaux de Diomède* as well as composing the English version of *Physique de l'amour*. It is notable, however, that *Une Nuit au Luxembourg* drifts nostalgically back to a more wholeheartedly sentimental view of womanhood, which is reclothed in a contentedly pagan religious imagery. It seems that his dreams became more of a consolation to him as his long exile progressed, and that he was forced in the end to a lachrymose lamentation of the evil circumstances which

94

had thwarted his ambition fully to complement the education of *les livres* with that of *l'amour*.

* * * * * * *

Gourmont's attitudes to the world in general may be seen as an extension of his attitudes to sex. Early in his career, under the influence of Schopenhauer, he became an out-and-out idealist, and found the rejection of materialism liberating. In *Le Livre des masques* (1896), he summed up his position thus:

> The world is my representation. I do not see what is; what is, is what I see. So many thinking men, so many and perhaps different worlds. This doctrine, which Kant left on the way to go to the assistance of shipwrecked morality, is so beautiful and so supple that it can be transposed without harming free logic from theory to even the most exacting practice, a universal principle of emancipation for every man capable of understanding it.[4]

The intellectual liberation which Gourmont derived from such ideas is perhaps most extravagantly displayed in *Le Chemin de velours* (1902), whose velvet path is strewn with slick quasi-Nietzschean aphorisms; Christianity is "a machine for creating remorse, because it is a machine for diminishing the subtlety, and for restraining the spontaneity, of vital reactions," while human intelligence, "far from being the object of creation, is only an accident," and moral ideas "are merely vegetable parasites born from an excess of nutrition."[5]

Such comments as these demonstrate that Gourmont's journey into solitude, however much it may have been forced upon him, was a bold and determined one, and that he carried in his intellectual baggage instruments for the amelioration of his condition. He cut himself off not merely from his social and religious heritage, but also from those aspects of contemporary philosophy which were useless to him—but the pride he took in being an individual, a man apart in every possible way, demanded respect with an ironically seigneurial hauteur.

Gourmont earned that respect—to the extent that Anatole France once referred to him as "the greatest living French writer"—with both the quality of his scholarship and the individuality of his outlook. He became the leading literary critic of his day, not merely by the breadth of his reading and the penetration of his intelligence, but also because he had a unique sympathy with many of the writers whose reputations he helped to establish and secure. He understood better than any other commentator the profound feelings of disenchantment, cynicism, and alienation which the writers of the *fin de siècle* inherited from Baudelaire and Lautréamont, and elevated as bloody banners of their own triumphant distress.

Gourmont cannot have considered himself—as some others certainly did consider him—to have been a man "born out of his time." We know this because he poured scorn on the very idea. In a memoir of Villiers de L'Isle-Adam published in *Le Livre des masques*, he cited such judgments as instances of "disturbed admiration," and opined that calling a man a genius was a recognition that he must be reckoned a synthetic product of his race and his epoch: "the brain and mouth of a whole tribe [rather than] a transient monster." But Gourmont was never afraid of apparent contradictions, especially if they were suitably ironic, and he came close to delivering some such judgment himself a mere two years later, in *Le Deuxième livre des masques* (1898), when he turned his attention to the work of a less celebrated writer. It is difficult to believe, reading what he wrote then, that he could have passed any other judgment on his own life or his own work:

> Some men are not in harmony with their time; they never live with the life of the people; the soul of crowds does not seem to them very superior to the soul of herds. If one of these men reflects on himself and comes to understand himself and to place himself in the vast world, he may grow sad, for about him he feels an invincible stretch of indifference, a mute Nature, stupid stones, geometrical movements; a great social solitude. And from the depths of his ennui he thinks of the simple pleasure of being in harmony, of laughing naturally, of smiling in an unreserved way, of being moved by long commotions. But there may come to him a pride in his renunciation and his isolation, whether he has adopted the pose of a pillar-hermit or whether he has shut the gates of a palace on his pleasures.[6]

VIII.

THE TORTURE GARDEN:

OCTAVE MIRBEAU AND THE POLITICS OF DECADENCE

No wholehearted Decadent is interested in politics, because practical politics is essentially progressive; it looks forward to a productive transformation of the world. Joséphin Péladan cannot qualify as an authentic Decadent because he believed—or pretended to believe—that the world might be saved from its sink of corruption by magic. Anatole France cannot qualify as an authentic Decadent, in spite of his crucial contributions to Literary Satanism, because he never surrendered hope for the renewal of the world, ultimately nailing his colors to the mast of communism. True Decadents like Jean Lorrain had political attitudes, usually of a Romantically conservative stripe, but they were outspoken in despising and deriding the sordid business of government.

There is, however, another kind of political thought which is defiantly impractical, embodying fierce and scathing criticism of existent political structures without feeling compelled to produce alternative constitutions and mechanisms of administration. If it were possible for a Decadent to have a political creed at all, that political creed would be anarchism. Anarchism is compatible with the Decadent consciousness in holding and boldly asserting that all the laws and law-making institutions of the modern world are corrupt to the point of putrefaction; it diverges only when it demands active revolution as a cure. The anarchist who contents himself with the contemplation of social evils, even if he consoles himself with fantasies of social collapse, will be recognized as a kindred spirit by the most diehard Decadent—even one whose illusions of noble descent render him utterly contemptuous of the masses.

Given this, it is not entirely surprising that the work which deserves to be reckoned the ultimate allegory of the Decadent worldview was produced by an anarchist: Octave Mirbeau's *Le Jardin des supplices* (1899). It grew out of a biographical and literary context which is in some ways strikingly different from Lorrain's and Gourmont's, but which is therefore all the more interesting in respect of its touching-points.

* * * * * * *

Octave Mirbeau was born in Trevières—a small town in Normandy—in Europe's year of revolutions, 1848. From his family he inherited the conservative bourgeois values of the rural middle class. These values were supposed to be solidly cemented by the Jesuits, to whom he was sent for schooling in 1859, but his sufferings at their hands were so humiliating that they had an opposite effect, sowing seeds of furious resentment. His rebellion was not immediate; like Lorrain and Gourmont he set out to study the law, and like them he went to Paris to pursue his studies. Unlike them, though, he served as an officer in the Army of the Loire during the Franco-Prussian War, tasting violence and defeat, and it was this experience which turned him away from his projected career.

A family friend found Mirbeau a job as art critic for the Bonapartist newspaper, *L'Ordre*. Once he had taken his place in the literary community of the nation, however, he began to reformulate his values and began a drift to radicalism which ultimately became a determined charge. Mirbeau's career paralleled in many significant features that of his near-contemporary Anatole France, who had been born in 1844. Like France he abandoned his conservative heritage to embrace a fierce radicalism, became extraordinarily passionate in his anti-clericalism, and was numbered among the most outspoken supporters of the ill-fated Captain Dreyfus. France's literary career was, however, launched from the groves of Academe, while Mirbeau's set out from the platform of popular journalism, and their literary armaments were of a markedly different character.

France's anti-clericalism was first given free rein in the short novel "La Tragédie humaine" (1895), in which a genuinely virtuous priest is bitterly disappointed to discover that the only mercy and charity to be found in a world dominated by the hopelessly-corrupt Church is the compassion of Satan. No stronger contrast can be imagined, given the basic similarity of feeling, than that between France's neat and poignant fable and Mirbeau's novel *L'Abbé Jules* (1888), which offers a complex and somewhat paradoxical portrait of its eponymous anti-hero, who is a veritable monster. Mirbeau's clear intention was to demonstrate that the abominable Jules is really a victim of society, a mirror of the corruption inherent in his environment, but the achievement of this end was subverted by the grotesque exaggeration which he used to melodramatize his argument. To be widely misunderstood because of his extravagance was to be Mirbeau's perennial burden.

The literary work which represented the culmination of France's radicalism was *La Révolte des anges* (1914), in which a young idealist among the fallen angels—whose elder counterparts have long been the tutors and comforters of mankind—sets out to raise an army of revolution against the tyrant demiurge who has set himself up as God, and searches for Satan in the hope of finding a general fit to lead the campaign. Typically, France's novel ends quietly, when Satan—who has been following the advice which Voltaire offered at the end of *Candide* by cultivating his garden—declines to play the Napoleonic role, on the grounds that were the battle to be won he would only end up (as Napoléon did) as a vainglorious emperor, no better than the king who had been toppled. On the surface, at least, there is little which this witty, urbane, and sentimental book has in common with Mirbeau's *Le Jardin des supplices*, but at heart they share the same motives: to expose the hypocrisies of Church and society; to shock the reader into a realization that much of what he or she complacently takes for granted is really cruel and ugly.

The difference between the delicacy of France—who was always at his most punctilious when dealing with implicitly shocking premises—and the luridness of Mirbeau is a matter of method. France's method won him the Nobel Prize, while Mirbeau's created sufficient embarrassment to have his work condemned as obscene, but that should not be allowed to obscure the fact their accomplishments were not so very unalike. Mirbeau's rhetoric proved a little too effective for his own good, both in his own lifetime and afterwards; but the undermining of his literary reputation—the amount of space devoted to Mirbeau in reference books in no way does justice to his contemporary importance as a force within the French literary community—has little to do with the aesthetic merit of his books or the moral weight of his arguments. He is a writer of considerable power and originality, who is one of the most striking and most interesting products of the great French tradition of philosophical fiction.

****

Whereas 1884 was the crucial year for authors central to the Decadent Movement, it was 1885 that marked the turning point of Mirbeau's life. That was the year in which French versions appeared of two works which were to have an enormous impact on his ideas about life and literature: Kropotkin's *Paroles d'un révolté* and Tolstoy's *Ma religion*. Both helped to give form and force to Mirbeau's developing anarchism, and the second—although it failed to shake the dogmatic atheism which he had adopted in opposition to the Jesuits—made him think long and hard about the ideological functions of literature. His journalistic pieces became much more outspoken in the defense of writers and artists under attack—1885 was also the year in which a storm blew up over the the government's censorship of the stage version of Zola's *Germinal*.

Mirbeau was already involved in ongoing controversies regarding the poetry of Symbolists, the painting of Impressionists and the novels of Naturalists. He had long been a friend of Maupassant and Zola, and had been a significant early champion of Monet, Gauguin, and Rodin. Now he was ready and willing to rally to the cause of anyone who attracted the ire of the establishment—even aristocrats like Rémy de Gourmont.

Until 1885 the shape of Mirbeau's journalistic career was broadly similar to that of his fellow Norman, Jean Lorrain; both were basically critics of art and literature whose wider explorations of "modern culture" took the form of sarcastic destructive criticism with no particular political complexion. In that year, though, Mirbeau gave up writing for the monarchist paper *Le Gaulois*, and went to the radical *La France* in order to launch a vitriolic attack upon the penal code (which is recapitulated in some of the more savagely sarcastic passages of *Le Jardin des supplices*). His fiction had also paralleled Lorrain's in its development, mostly taking the form of rather derivative short stories. While Lorrain remained obsessed with sexual perversity and the supernatural, however, Mirbeau began to develop a naturalistic species of *contes cruels*. His collection *Lettres de ma chaumière* was both intensely personal and stridently polemical, reflecting vitriolically on the life and folkways of Normandy.

This mixture of the autobiographical and the polemical was carried to greater lengths in Mirbeau's first novel, *Le Calvaire* (1886), where the bitterness of his reflections on the iniquities of social injustice are compounded by the emotional residues of an unhappy love affair. The novel proved controversial because of the way in which Mirbeau transformed his own experiences of the Franco-Prussian war into a savage condemnation of military stupidity which seemed anti-patriotic to many (the relevant chapter was dropped from the serial version for that reason), but its most remarkable feature is the portrayal of its chief female character, whose seduction, betrayal, mental torture, ruination, and final abandonment of the hero constitutes the slow crucifixion to which the title refers.

The misogynistic subtext of this characterization links *Le Calvaire* to the fascination which many of the leading figures of the Decadent Movement had with *femmes fatales*. One of Mirbeau's closest friends was Barbey d'Aurevilly, whose *Les Diaboliques* (1874) had elaborately displayed the conviction that the façades of social convention and politeness conceal awesome depths of moral depravity, and that women in particular have become expert in using the mask of virtue to obscure a murderous callousness. In the same year that Mirbeau published *Le Calvaire*, Villiers de L'Isle-Adam published his extraordinary *L'Eve future*, in which a nobleman disappointed by the appalling perfidies of womankind commissions Thomas Edison to manufacture a beautiful machine which will embody all the virtues of fidelity and love of which real women seem to be incapable.

Mirbeau followed *Le Calvaire* and *Abbé Jules* with the explicitly political novel *Sébastien Roch* (1890), which offered a minutely-detailed retrospective analysis of his experiences at the Jesuit college at Vannes which he had attended in infancy. The ruination of the novel's hero is much more complete than Mirbeau's own spoliation—the nightmarish hangover of his "education" drives Roch to an early grave—but this tragedy is compounded by the fact that within the beleaguered mind of the youth a rebellion of compassionate feeling has begun to take shape, only to be cruelly aborted. As in his previous novels, Mirbeau derived affective force from a recapitulation of his early tribulations which omits any record of his own eventual redemption; a noticeable discrepancy thus opened up between the apparent pessimism of his fiction and the relative optimism of his political articles.

Discrepancies of this kind are not uncommon, and are frequently misunderstood; the fact that the rhetoric of fiction is fundamentally alarmist has as much to do with the essential nature of dramatic tension than the attitudes of writers. All Utopian fiction is weak and anemic; whatever its virtues as a form of political analysis, it has none as engaging narrative. By contrast, dystopian accounts of nightmarish alternative worlds often constitute eloquent and powerful statements of what is wrong with the world.

* * * * * * *

Although *Le Jardin des supplices* was not published in full until 1899, it drew upon some earlier materials, and Mirbeau may have begun work on it as early as 1892. It seems, however, that it was his involvement in the Dreyfus affair between 1896 and 1898 which confirmed his determination to write a more scathing attack on the hypocrisies and injustices of French society than any which had gone before. Unlike Anatole France's similarly-motivated *L'Ile des pingouins* (1908), Mirbeau's novel contains very few overt references to the injustice of the treatment meted out to the luckless captain; but the text's scalding sarcasm when it deals with the hideous callousness and injustice of the workings of the law and its human instruments embodies a particular fury which the case certainly helped to awaken. The form and manner of the novel might have been determined before, but it was the Dreyfus Affair which provided the fervent impetus necessary for its completion.

It is probable that Mirbeau had found *Le Jardin des supplices* very difficult to write because it was the first of his novels to break away—and the only one to break away entirely—from the autobiographical resources which had fuelled his earlier work. It is the most artificial and the most self-consciously literary of his works, and it embodies a keen awareness of the various literary traditions to which it belongs, which include the tradition of the critical *conte philosophique* developed by Voltaire and Diderot, as well as the tradition of French Orientalism which was the common property of the Romantic and Decadent Movements.

In its basic construction, *Le Jardin des supplices* echoes—probably quite deliberately—the form of Thomas More's *Utopia*. Where More's book had an introductory letter introducing its narrator, Mirbeau's has a preface introducing "the manuscript." More's book then presents a dialogue in which contemporary society is subject to various criticisms, before moving into its partly satirical and partly homiletic account of the imaginary island of Utopia. Mirbeau likewise divides his main story into two, first presenting a satirical examination of contemporary society via an abbreviated autobiography of the author of the manuscript, then moving on to a detailed description of the allegorical Garden of Tortures, which the narrator discovers in China in the company of his remarkable mistress, Clara.

Le Jardin des supplices is frequently represented as a work which owes much to the Marquis de Sade, and Clara has been deemed the perfect exemplar of a connoisseur of Sadism. There are indeed certain affinities between *Le Jardin des supplices* and some passages to be found in *Juliette*, because the method of both works requires detailed description of particularly nasty methods of torture and execution, but these similarities are compounded with vitally important differences, and the philosophical discourses to which the two writers affiliate their arguments are quite distinct.

The argument of Sade's *Juliette*, reduced to its simplest possible form, is that once we accept that there is no God, then the foundation-stone of human morality has been removed. If there is no God to reward us with salvation or punish us with eternal damnation, Sade's characters argue, then what good reason can we possibly have for preferring good to evil? Is it not the case, they propose, that once the fear of retribution is eliminated, then the decision is merely a matter of taste—of arbitrary aesthetic preference?

As has been previously noted, Sade is providing a challenge to convention rather than drawing a conclusion, dramatizing a problem rather than issuing a manifesto. There is, however, an element of special pleading in his work; Sade found himself to be sexually stimulated by the contemplation of various forms of behavior usually considered perverse and/or disgusting, and by lurid fantasies of extreme violence. Like others so afflicted, he was both fascinated by and anxious about this curious susceptibility.

To what extent Sade could or did import the substance of these fantasies into his actual behavior we cannot be sure, but it is probably safe to assume that like everyone else in the world his real accomplishments had very little connection with his daydreams. Although people occasionally do try to act out their fantasies—sexual and otherwise—in a spirit of extreme optimism, they invariably find that reality cannot match the vivid promise of fantasy. Much of the excitement of fantasy derives from the fact that it *is* fantasy, and that it has all the power of the imagination to draw upon in envisaging an impossibly gorgeous and sensual experience which mere mundanity could never offer. The alchemy of fantasy permits excitement to be isolated and miraculously purified, while the mere chemistry which cannot be excluded from actual sexual intercourse and the actual cruelties of bullying and other assorted blood sports insists upon compounding it with the vagaries of physiology, with dirt, with discomfort, and with injury—and thus, alas, with matters of pragmatic morality from which fantasy can easily be freed. The only way in which fantasy can sensibly enter actual behavior is as play; whenever the acting out become serious it tends to become ridiculous, and perhaps also dangerous.

Mirbeau was, like Sade, a committed atheist—but he lived in an age where atheism was less implicitly outrageous. In Sade's day the desertion of faith carried an inevitable sensation of implicit wickedness, with which Sade coped by declaring it to be delicious. For Mirbeau, atheism was something which could simply be embraced and then taken for granted. There was for him, as for Anatole France and Jules Michelet, no particular difficulty in considering religion—and therefore the object of religious worship—as a recognizable evil in itself. For Mirbeau and his contemporaries the death of God did not imply that the very notion of morality must be thrown overboard; on the contrary, it was in part the perception of a better and truer morality which had contrived to throw God overboard.

What was for Sade a fascinating and difficult problem—how to construct a secular morality—was for Mirbeau a matter to be taken very much for granted. He knew perfectly well what Good was—it was compassion and fairness—and that Evil was its negation; what seemed to him to be fascinating, appalling, and desperately problematic was that in civilized society there was so much Evil masquerading as Good, which the majority of people seemed not even to see, let alone to care about. In *Le Jardin des supplices*, therefore, he set out to show people what their world, behind its careful façades and hypocrisies, was truly like. He employed analytical discussion (in the preface), satirical caricature (in the first part of the main narrative), and fantastic allegory (in the second part of the main narrative) in order to strip away all the masks and illusions of custom and philosophy, thus displaying all the callousness and perversity of the underlying psyche of "civilized" man.

Where Sade had set out slyly to create moral unease, therefore, Mirbeau set out forthrightly to call forth moral outrage. Like Sade before him, though, he could not do so without calling attention to the mysterious attractiveness of images of painful perversity. It is perfectly obvious to any reader of *Le Jardin des supplices* that Mirbeau, like

Sade, is something of a connoisseur of such imagery, interested in understanding its hold over his own imagination and its power as a generator of private fantasies. It is, therefore, a study in the alchemy of fantasy as well as a condemnation of the hidden brutality of civilized mores, and this is what places its investigations at the heart of the Decadent Quest, carrying forward that mission to explore the remotest depths of human passion which—according to Jean Des Esseintes—Baudelaire had so boldly pioneered.

The true kernel of *Le Jardin des supplices*, seen from this angle, is the relationship between the narrator and the mistress whom he meets while going into exile. The narrator, like other Mirbeau antiheroes, is a typically-corrupt product of a society in which all moral authority—parental, educational, juridical, and political—is a mere show, the one true motive in human affairs being the determination to "get the better of people." This narrator, however, is an utter incompetent; although he allies himself early in life with the cynical Eugène Mortain, who rises to become a Minister of France, he remains a mere pawn, pathetically unable to take advantage of the opportunities for personal advancement which are presented to him. When he has become an embarrassment to his one-time friend, he is persuaded to pass himself off as a scientist in order that he might pursue his supposed researches in Ceylon. His subsequent meeting with Clara, who persuades him to go with her to China instead, is a crucial diversion from the geographical Orient to the exotic Orient of the French literary imagination.

The significance of this imaginary Orient to French writers of the nineteenth century—and by no means only those of a Romantic stripe—can hardly be underestimated. The documentary accounts of actual exotica produced by such writers as Gérard de Nerval and Pierre Loti, though popular, could not compare with the lush Orient of the imagination which was celebrated by Théophile Gautier and—in a more genteel but more elaborate fashion—by his daughter Judith in such works as *Le Dragon impérial* (1869) and *Iskender* (1886). The further the imaginative spectrum extended eastwards, the lusher and gaudier its imagery became, and Mirbeau elected to extend it to a new limit.

It is through the monstrous but extremely seductive Clara that Mirbeau's narrator is eventually brought to confront the true nature of the forces which have shaped him—not only in the population and configuration of the Garden to which she takes him, but in her voyeuristic response to it. The catalogue of cruelties through which she escorts the narrator (and the reader) arouses such an erotic fervor that her visit culminates in a kind of orgasm. The aftermath of this discharge is allegedly cathartic, leaving her not merely sated but somewhat repentant; it is, however, obvious that this is a temporary state of affairs, and that the inadequacy of her run-of-the-mill erotic experiences will ultimately drive her back to the garden.

The garden of tortures represents, of course, the ultimate display of Baudelaire's "flowers of evil." Des Esseintes's collection of horrid hothouse flowers, and the hallucinatory dream occasioned thereby, were used by Huysmans to symbolize the role of syphilis in human affairs, but Mirbeau has something much more expansive in mind. His flowers of evil reflect all the horrors of human nature and conduct. Their effect on Clara is overwhelming, and her submission to their authority may be interpreted as the Decadent's capitulation with the deceptive seductions of luxury, but the narrator cannot share her total immersion; his reaction is quite different:

> I feel something like a powerful oppression, like an immense fatigue after marching and marching across fever-laden jungles, or by the shores of deadly lakes....and I am flooded by discouragement, so that it seems I shall never be able to escape from myself again. At the same time, my brain is heavy and troubles me. I feel as though an iron band were clasping my temples, tight enough to burst my skull.
>
> Then, little by little, my thoughts abandon the garden, the torture-arenas, the agony beneath the bell, the trees haunted by pain, the bloody and devouring flowers. They are trying to burst through the setting of this charnel-house, penetrate to pure light, knock once more upon the gates of life. Alas, the gates of life never swing open except upon death, never open except upon the palaces and gardens of death. And the universe appears to me like an immense, inexorable torture-garden. Blood everywhere and, where there is most life, horrible tormentors who dig your flesh, saw your bones, and retract your skin with sinister, joyful faces.
>
> Ah yes! the Torture Garden! Passions, appetites, greed, hatred and lies; law, social institutions, justice, love, glory, heroism, and religion: these are its monstrous flowers and its hideous instruments of eternal human suffering. What I saw today, and what I heard, exists and cries and howls beyond this garden, which is no more than a symbol to me of the entire earth. I have vainly sought a respite in quietude and repose in death, and I can find them nowhere.[1]

The experience of the garden is too much for the narrator to bear; his reaction is one of outright horror, but the impulse that horror instills in him is flight rather than rebellion. The reawakened Clara finds his weeping and wailing annoying and pathetic; she is impatient with his cowardice. She is undoubtedly correct in her judgment that the seeds of a similar corruption are within him, and would surely have germinated were it not for his simple incompetence in the business of getting the better of people. Throughout the concluding pages of the novel the narrator's sole recourse is to repeat her name over and over again, in the desperate and demeaning hope that her erotic attentions might serve to blind him to everything he has seen and everything he has learned. The reader is tacitly invited to weigh the moral quality of his or her own response.

* * * * * * *

Mirbeau published four more novels after *Le Jardin des supplices*: *Le Journal d'une femme de chambre* (1900): *Les Vingt-et-un jours d'un neurasthénique* (1901); *La 628-E8* (1907), and *Dingo* (1913). Another, *Un Gentilhomme*, was published posthumously in 1920, three years after his death. The first of these is the work for which he is nowadays best-known, partly by virtue of Jean Renoir's 1946 film starring Jean Moreau. Like *Le Jardin des supplices* it tends to be regarded as a semi-pornographic work, because it attempts to repeat the same message in a more realistic mode. It follows the adventures of a young girl as she bears witness to the depravity of a sequence of exploitative employers, becoming gradually more cynical as she does so, ultimately—and inevitably—ending up as corrupt as they are.

Le Journal d'une femme de chambre has at least as much in common with Sade's *Justine* and *Juliette* as *Le Jardin des supplices* has, because it shares the same models, a group of English novels: Daniel Defoe's *Moll Flanders* (1722), Samuel Richardson's *Pamela; or, Virtue Rewarded* (1740-41), and John Cleland's *Memoirs of a Woman of Pleasure* (1749), better known as *Fanny Hill*. It was Richardson's piously moralistic novel which Sade—with an altogether appropriate sense of paradox—gleefully took as his exemplar, carefully inverting its subtitle. (*Justine* is subtitled *les malheurs de la vertu*; *Juliette* is called *les prospérités du vice*). All the earlier writers were, however, seduced by their heroines in a way that Mirbeau never was; how much his detachment owed to his misogyny and how much to his political objectivity it is difficult to say, but the fact remains that he was much more clinically analytical in his study of Célestine's strategies for coping with the oppressive demands of men and the world than any of his predecessors.

In the next two "novels" this clinicality is taken to such lengths that the books become collections of caricatures in prose, each presenting a grotesque gallery of perverse characters without any semblance of a plot. Individual character-studies taken from them have occasionally been reprinted as *contes cruels*. The "neurasthenic" whose observations at a health spa form the text of the *Les Vingt-et-un jours d'un neurasthénique* has certain symptoms in common with the Duc de Fréneuse, but he gets little sympathy from his creator on that account; he comes across as a mere hypochondriac whose malaise hardly requires palliation, let alone a cure. This consistent lack of sympathy for his viewpoint characters has a marked distancing effect which differentiates Mirbeau's analyses of social corruption from those of writers closer to the heart of the Decadent Movement, but it also gives them a cutting edge which more self-indulgent writers lacked.

Dingo goes even further than its predecessors in this respect, taking as its viewpoint character a dog which proves ultimately untamable in spite of the efforts of its human masters to teach it civilized ways. Mirbeau uses this figure to present a deeply ironic and calculatedly perverse self-image which bears no resemblance at all to Huysmans's Des Esseintes or Lorrain's Duc de Fréneuse. Interestingly, this last novel offers portraits of a few of its human characters rather more sympathetic than any Mirbeau had ever offered before. Although it is obvious throughout what the dog's eventual fate must be, this is in many ways the author's most sympathetic and most hopeful novel.

Perhaps Mirbeau was right to see himself as a kind of metaphorical wild dog, ultimately unassimilable by society, because it could not contain or control the rage engendered by his instinct for natural justice. If so, it was not so much that he was a radical, but that he was so bad-tempered about it. Had he been as slick and polished as Anatole France, his work would have been more widely applauded and more widely liked. Even those whose own ideological views are utterly opposed to those of *La Révolte des anges* can find it an agreeable book to read, and a book full of nourishing food for thought, but *Le Jardin des supplices*—and almost everything else that Mirbeau wrote—was calculated to be provocatively disagreeable and essentially indigestible.

Those who disliked Mirbeau accused him of being a hypocrite because he maintained a comfortable lifestyle while preaching anarchism. He was aware of the anomaly himself, and was perfectly capable of caricaturing himself in his novels alongside all his other targets, but he was enough of a Decadent never to think of giving up his comforts for the sake of his cause. At the end of the day his cause remained a matter of loud complaint and clever abuse, but he understood what he was abusing well enough to provide, in *Le Jardin des supplices*, one of the finest accounts of a world that was genuinely out of the world, while reflecting with appalling clarity the manner in which the compost of contemporary civilization provided the perfect matrix for *les fleurs du mal*.

IX.

THE DECAY OF LYING:

OSCAR WILDE AND THE
ENGLISH DECADENT MOVEMENT

What passed for Decadence in England was but a pale shadow of French Decadence. In the eyes of upright Victorians all French literature seemed dreadfully decadent, and "decadent" was freely bandied about as a term of abuse which carried a distinctly xenophobic implication. The idea of historical and cultural decadence never acquired, in England, the same specific connotations which it had in France; despite Gibbon's amplification of Montesquieu's arguments, the term was not tied to the idea of failing and falling empires; rather it was used— promiscuously, one might say—to refer to moral license and moral laxness.

Such was the English attitude to Paris that "French" and "decadent" were virtually synonymous in certain realms of discourse. The Rev. W. F. Barry contributed two articles to the *Quarterly Review* in 1890 and 1892 entitled "Realism and Decadence in French Literature" and "The French Decadence," under which titles he subsumed discussion of writers as varied as Balzac, Zola, Maupassant, and Daudet, all of whom he found morally suspect by the standards of British neo-Puritanism.

The customary subject-matter of run-of-the-mill Decadent novels would have been considered so indecent by any contemporary British publisher as to be quite unpublishable. Poetry was granted far more latitude, but Swinburne was widely considered to be a highly inappropriate role model. Inevitably, though, there were English writers whose attitude to Paris was very different from that of the puritan Establishment. It was not so very difficult to see Victorianism as a worldview in decay, which could not and ought not to survive the death of its decrepit figurehead. Such writers saw in the salons and Bohemian circles of Paris an enthusiasm, freedom of expression, and stylishness which were entirely enviable. As an avant garde, however, they had to deal with Britain as it was, and they had no alternative in the beginning but to import the Decadent style with only the merest shadow of its substance.

The would-be champion of English Decadence was Arthur Symons, who was willing enough to wear the label until it became too great an embarrassment, and who urged others to wear it too. His essay on "The Decadent Movement in Literature," published in *Harper's New Monthly Magazine* in 1893, begins by regretting the confusion of terms currently being deployed in the hope of capturing the essence of the major currents in European art, and admits that Decadence overlaps somewhat with Symbolism and Impressionism. Symons asserts, however, that the notion of Decadence best captures the temper of the work, which he is happy to accept as "a new and beautiful and interesting disease." The character of the new art, he argues, echoes the character of the art produced by the Greek and Latin cultures in their senescence; his description of it includes: "intense self-consciousness...restless curiosity...an over subtilizing refinement upon refinement, a spiritual and moral perversity."

All of this Symons was initially enthusiastic to take aboard. The writers he offers as the most meritorious contemporary exemplars of the Movement are Verlaine, Huysmans, and the Belgian playwright Maurice Maeterlinck. In the first version of the essay Symons named Walter Pater and W. E. Henley as significant English proto-Decadents, but he removed the references for diplomatic reasons when the essay was reprinted in book form.

Symons was a member of the Rhymers' Club, which met at an eating house in Fleet Street; his fellow members included Ernest Dowson, Lionel Johnson, John Davidson, Richard Le Gallienne, and William Butler Yeats. Some of these agreed with Symons sufficiently to allow a measure of Decadent influence into their work, and none of them entirely escaped guilt by association, but if it is to be reckoned as the spearhead of an English Decadent Movement their work is distinctly half-hearted. Fugitive Decadent elements are easy enough to find in the work of Johnson and Yeats, but only Dowson, apart from Symons himself, was really significantly affected by the Decadent attitude. In Dowson's case this influence was greatly assisted by his infection with the tuberculosis which drove both his parents to suicide, but his marginally Decadent work is far more melancholy than morbid; the paradoxical thrill of perversity which so entranced the French Decadents is not to be found there.

None of the Rhymers ever lost sight, even temporarily, of aesthetic ideals which might give their work some kind of uplifting quality, and most retained their religious faith as well. In addition, they exhibited a tendency, even when they condescended to take Decadence seriously, not to take it *too* seriously. Lionel Johnson's essay on "The Cultured Faun" in the *Anti-Jacobin* (1891) offers a portrait of the contentedly neurasthenic artist which is nine parts parody. If one compares such poems by Symons as "The Opium-Smoker" (in *Days and Nights*, 1889) and "The Absinthe-Drinker" (in *Silhouettes*, 1892) with the rhapsodies of Gautier, Baudelaire, and Farrère they seem dreadfully anemic. Symons translated a good deal of French Decadent poetry into English, but his translations of Baudelaire and Rimbaud now seem enervatingly prettified.

* * * * * * *

Just as the French Decadents had inherited a doctrine of art for art's sake from Gautier, so the Rhymers and their contemporaries inherited one from Swinburne and the Pre-Raphaelites, elaborately mapped out by Walter Pater. Pater's exemplary *Marius the Epicurean* is, however, a man of far greater austerity, decorum, and moral rectitude than the pagans of French fiction, and the English art which was done for English art's sake was similarly constrained. The lush exoticism and calculated gaudiness of French Romanticism and Orientalism is nowhere to be found. Swinburne sometimes achieved an admirably feverish intensity, reflected in the rhythm as well as the imagery of his poems, but his imagery was diluted by sheer verbosity.

Like the most nearly-Decadent of the Pre-Raphaelites, Dante Gabriel Rossetti, Swinburne was looked after by Theodore Watts-Dunton when his lifestyle made him ill; whether this benevolence may have softened the splenetic tendencies of his work must remain a matter for conjecture. Eugene Lee-Hamilton, who warrants inclusion among British proto-Decadents, spent twenty years as a chronic (possibly psychosomatic) invalid, but was apparently saved from undue bitterness by a thoroughly British expectation that it was simply not done to be too self-indulgent in one's misery. From *The New Medusa* (1882) to *Sonnets of the Wingless Hours* (1895), his work toyed incessantly with Decadent images, but it always retained a measure of reserve which was echoed in real life when, after publication of the latter collection, he made a complete recovery from his illness. Lee-Hamilton did, however, go on to write a phantasmagorical historical novel, *The Lord of the Dark Red Star* (1903), whose vivid imagery recalls the French historical fantasies peripheral to the Decadent Movement, and his half-sister Violet Paget—who signed herself Vernon Lee—incorporated similar elements into some of her own historical fantasies.

Those Rhymers most closely associated with Symons's Decadent propaganda could lay claim to equally adequate neurasthenic symptoms, and they mostly died young as a result of their various ailments. Dowson died at thirty-three, having spent his last years as an exile in France. Lionel Johnson was an alcoholic who eventually became a recluse and died at thirty-five. Even Symons contrived to suffer a nervous breakdown in 1908 (when he was forty-three), was certified insane, and was diagnosed as suffering from "general paralysis" (a term usually employed as a euphemism for syphilis), but he defied fate and his doctors by recovering and surviving to the ripe old age of eighty. Others whose fates might be added to this catalogue of misfortunes include John Davidson, who hurled himself from a cliff at fifty-two, having been deeply affected by Nietzschean ideas of the redundancy of contemporary man, and a writer very heavily influenced by Davidson, James Elroy Flecker, who died of tuberculosis at thirty-one.

Flecker was born too late to be labelled a Decadent—his first volume of poems was published in 1907—but his career followed a course mapped out by countless French writers, including a voyage to the Orient whose legacy had a powerful effect on his later work, most notably the long narrative poem *The Golden Journey to Samarkand* (from whose first draft the homoerotic elements were dutifully removed before publication). He produced the first English version of Baudelaire's "Litany to Satan," and his novelette *The Last Generation* (1908) is a fine sarcastic fantasy in which the people of the near future, accepting the Decadence of their culture, neglect the production of children and thus ensure its mortality.

Despite all these stigmata the English Decadents never subscribed to a medicated theory of artistic creativity in the way that so many of the French Decadents came to do. They did have medical men associated with the movement—most notably Havelock Ellis, whose pre-Freudian investigations of the psychology of sex were a significant, if soon outdated, contribution to the development of human science—but Ellis's proto-psychology could not find room for the follies of Moreau de Tours and Lombroso, and his literary criticism was in any case much more closely associated with his philosophical interests. Like Davidson, Ellis was fascinated by Nietzsche, who was too positive a thinker to license any kind of languorous self-indulgence. When writing as a literary critic, Ellis was also enthusiastic to use the cautionary argument with which British Decadents habitually defended themselves against the pejorative implications of the word; his notable essay on Huysmans in *Affirmations* (1898) takes care to emphasize that Decadence ought to be viewed entirely as an aesthetic concept and not a moral one.

This insistence that English literary Decadence did not intend to be subversive of moral standards, and had nothing to do with morality at all, was so frequently reiterated by its supporters as to constitute an Ophelian excess of protestation. Its contemptuous paradoxicality was eventually put to the test in a court of law, but not in the relatively mild manner that had lent French Decadence a useful scandalous edge. Baudelaire and Jean Lorrain were charged with publishing obscenities and fined, but the central figure of the fledgling English Movement—the man who seemed to symbolize everything implicit in the word "Decadence"—was charged with gross indecency and sentenced to two years hard labor, which destroyed him utterly.

In a sense, English Decadence died the day sentence was passed on Oscar Wilde. The word was effectively discarded. Arthur Symons decided that his proposed book on *The Decadent Movement in Literature* would henceforth be known as *The Symbolist Movement in Literature*, under which title it eventually appeared in 1899. "It pleased some young men in various countries to call themselves Decadents," he noted in the introduction—evidently regretting if not actually forgetting that he had been one himself—

> with all the thrill of unsatisfied virtue masquerading as uncomprehended vice. As a matter of fact, the term is in its place only when applied to style.... No doubt perversity of form and perversity of matter are often found together, and, among lesser men especially, experiment was carried far, not only in the direction of style. But a movement which in this sense might be called Decadent could but have been a straying aside from the main road of literature. Nothing, not even conventional virtue, is so provincial as conventional vice.... The interlude, half a mock-interlude, of Decadence, diverted the attention of the critics while something more serious was in preparation. That something more serious has crystallized, for the time, under the form of Symbolism, in which art returns to the one pathway, leading through beautiful things to eternal beauty.[1]

That became the standard English view, relegating French Decadence to a transient fad and damning it with the worst insults imaginable: "provincial" and, even worse, "conventional." There is no chapter in Symons's book on Baudelaire, nor on Rémy de Gourmont, let alone Jean Lorrain. Even the chapter on Huysmans—which comes after those on Jules Laforgue and Mallarmé rather than before—is scrupulously entitled "The Later Huysmans," and concentrates almost exclusively on the novels written after his reconversion to religious faith, dismissing *A rebours* in one brief paragraph as a mere folly.

To a large extent, this remains the prevalent English view of the Decadent Movement, being only slightly modified in such interested but fundamentally dismissive studies as A. E. Carter's *The Idea of Decadence in French Literature, 1830-1900* (1958) and Jennifer Birkett's *The Sins of the Fathers: Decadence in France, 1870-1914* (1986). This is hardly surprising, given that even before Wilde's ritual crucifixion, attempts to make the ideas and ideals of Decadence acceptable to a British audience were beset by careful circumlocution and conscientious evasiveness. Nowhere is this argumentative sleight-of-hand more obvious, in fact, than in the writings of Wilde himself.

* * * * * * *

It is not until the tenth chapter of *The Picture of Dorian Gray* that the young anti-hero receives from Lord Henry Wootton the "yellow book" which becomes the foundation stone of his philosophy of life, but much of the groundwork for his conversion has already been laid. It is an earlier monologue of Lord Henry's—a hymn to Beauty—which inspires the fateful wish which allows Dorian to exchange personalities with his portrait, so that the unfading and timeless work of art becomes an actor in the real world while the portrait withers and festers in its frame. In this monologue Lord Henry emphasizes the full horror of what time will do to Dorian's awesome beauty, and insists—in the absence of any possible remedy—that it must be exploited to the full while it lasts. He advises the boy not to allow conventional morality to be his guide, but rather to devote himself to the search for new sensations. A new Hedonism, he says, is what the world needs, and he opines that Dorian might, with effort, become its "visible symbol."

That, indeed, is what Dorian—with effort—becomes.

A later passage in the text makes it clear that Lord Henry, like Des Esseintes, is essentially an experimenter; his opposition to all received wisdom is by way of subjecting it to a trial of fire, and his moulding of Dorian's character is supposedly a clinical exploration of possibility—his role is to play Frankenstein to Dorian's Monster rather than Mephistopheles to Dorian's Faust. The precise parallel which Lord Henry draws in comparing himself to a natural scientist is particularly revealing; he represents himself as a vivisectionist of human life, and expands his analogy in a fashion which is very similar to the way in which Des Esseintes extrapolates some of his analogies:

> It was true that as one watched life in its curious crucible of pain and pleasure, one could not wear over one's face a mask of glass, nor keep the sulphurous fumes from troubling the brain and making the imagination turbid with monstrous fancies and misshapen dreams. There were poisons so subtle that to know their properties one had to sicken of them. There were maladies so strange that one had to pass through them if one sought to understand their nature. And, yet, what a great reward one received! How wonderful the whole world became to one! To note the curious hard logic of passion, and the emotional colored life of the intellect—to observe where they met and where they separated, at what point they were in unison, and at what point they were at discord—there was a delight in that! What matter what the cost was?

One could never pay too high a price for any sensation.[2]

The next paragraph of this discourse makes art—and especially the art of literature—part and parcel of this discipline of experimental human science. A further extrapolation of the argument might represent the arts as instruments of this hypothetical psychological science, just as telescopes and microscopes are instruments of astronomy and anatomy.

If Lord Henry's viewpoint is accepted, there can be nothing surprising in his subsequent musings about the total irrelevance of moral considerations to the business of literature and to the experiment of remaking the character of Dorian Gray. Dorian's ill-fated love for the actress Sibyl Vane—which briefly threatens him with salvation by convention—is regarded only as an "interesting phenomenon," with no intrinsic value. In this harsh light the reason for the failure of that love becomes highly significant.

Dorian rejects Sibyl before he reads the infamous yellow book; it is entirely his own action, and even Lord Henry is surprised and slightly disturbed by it. Dorian falls out of love with Sybil because she loses her ability to act; it makes not the slightest difference to him that the reason that she loses her ability is that her love for him has awakened her to the reality of the world, and forced her to see it clearly, making dissimulation and pretence impossible. This makes it clear that the beauty which Dorian briefly discovered in Sybil was entirely the product of her artifice—he can find nothing to admire in her authenticity, and when she achieves it she becomes worthless to him. This is less surprising when one recalls that he has already traded his own authenticity for the ageless artifice of his portrait.

In view of what Dorian has elected to do to himself and to Sybil, it is entirely to be expected that he should find *A rebours* so absorbing and so appealing, and that he should be so enchanted by its "metaphors as monstrous as orchids, and as subtle in color." The yellow book is, Wilde's text candidly admits, a "poisonous book," which produces in its reader "a malady of dreaming," but neither "poisonous" nor "malady" can here be construed as a simple insult. Dorian deals with the book as Des Esseintes might have dealt with one of his own favorite texts: he procures nine copies of the first edition printed on especially sumptuous paper, and has them bound in different colors so that they might better suit his various moods. He recognizes in the story of Des Esseintes the story of his own life, which he has not yet lived.

There is, of course, one vital difference between Dorian and Des Esseintes: Dorian cannot exhibit the symptoms of sickness; he has delegated that misfortune to his portrait. He and he alone is fitted by his unique artifice successfully to live the Decadent life, untouchable by the ravages of incurable venereal disease. He is, of course, an impossible entity—every bit as impossible as that immortal soul in which Des Esseintes, Huysmans, Wilde, and Dorian himself all felt compelled to believe—but that only serves to make him all the more fascinating while he exists.

The conclusion of *The Picture of Dorian Gray* has no quack doctor to alarm Dorian with falsely melodramatic prognoses in the same way that Des Esseintes was alarmed, but it is a similar kind of anxiety which drives him (unnecessarily) onto the sharp horns of his dilemma. His determination to take a knife to his syphilitic image, lest it should somehow constitute "evidence" against him, is blatantly foolish and can only be interpreted as lamentable cowardice. Dorian's death provides a tidier ending than the blandly paradoxical commitment to faith which ends Des Esseintes's story, but it is by no means obvious that tidiness is to be reckoned virtuous in a text of this kind. If such a conclusion can be commended at all, it has to be be commended as a casual and thoroughly artificial flourish rather than as some sort of vindication of the vulgar opinion that natural law cannot in the end be cheated.

* * * * * *

Oscar Wilde's philosophy of art is more straightforwardly laid out in his essay on "The Decay of Lying," but even cast in non-fictional form it is teasingly and evasively removed from direct expression. "The Decay of Lying" is a comic dialogue between two characters called Vivian and Cyril (Wilde's two sons were named Cyril and Vyvyan); Vivian is writing an essay on "The Decay of Lying," from which he quotes liberally and upon which he comments in a fashion so arch that the reader is obliged to suppose that Wilde is making fun of him, even though he must also suspect that there are serious points being made.

Such stylistic contortionism is, of course, entirely in character: Wilde never could decide how seriously he intended his own poses, and he could not in the end refrain from slashing so savagely at his own carefully-crafted self-portrait as to bring destruction upon himself (if each man really is fated to kill the thing he loves, a hopeless libel action is evidently as effective a weapon as any).

The argument which is flippantly displayed in "The Decay of Lying" begins, in true Decadent fashion, with an attack on Nature. Wilde's sarcastic mouthpiece, Vivian, insists that Art has revealed to mankind the deficiencies of Nature: "[her] lack of design, her curious crudities, her extraordinary monotony, her absolutely unfinished condition." Art, he alleges, "is our spirited protest, our gallant attempt to teach nature her proper place." He goes on to stress the uncomfortableness of Nature, and its antipathy towards Mind; thinking, he proposes, can be seen as a kind of unhealthiness, as fatal as any other disease.

When Vivian goes on to reveal the title of the essay he is writing, his commonsensical friend Cyril protests that he sees no reason to think that lying is in decline, and that politicians seem to be keeping the tradition very much alive. Vivian counters with the argument that what politicians, journalists, and other everyday deceivers do is better regarded as mere misrepresentation; their efforts lack the magnitude and grandeur desirable in wholehearted lies. Lies, for Vivian, are a species of glorious fantasy which belong to the realm of Art, but for which contemporary artists have, alas, lost their appetite. Too many modern artists, Vivian laments, have fallen into slothful habits of truthfulness; their work has become representative instead of imaginative. Like Des Esseintes, he heaps scorn upon realism, with its tediously detailed studies of everyday vices and its insipid quest to expose "that dreadful universal thing called human nature"—and like Des Esseintes he is not afraid to name names and pulverize reputations.

Vivian continues to argue his case by documenting, in considerable detail, the oft-quoted Wildean claim that "Life imitates art far more than Art imitates life." Cyril challenges him to prove also that Nature imitates Art, and he rises instantly to the challenge, arguing that we must be taught to see such things as "landscapes" and "fogs" by artistic celebrations of the way they play with light and color. Although he stops short of stating that our idea of "Nature" is itself a kind of fantasy, it is not clear that he needs to.

Having said all this, Vivian returns to his argument that the art of lying is in a state of dereliction. The nineteenth century, he argues, is "the dullest and most prosaic century possible" (he had not experienced the twentieth!), and suggests that even the dreams which afflict the sleep of the middle classes have become tedious. He attacks the Church of England, as Des Esseintes attacks the Church of Rome, for losing sight of the supernatural and the mystical and becoming reasonable.

Some of Vivian's subsequent prescriptions for reviving the art of lying are more tongue-in-cheek than his destructive arguments, commending the good work which is done at dinner-parties and in the ordinary processes of education, but insisting that there remains much room for further improvement. Perhaps he is more serious, although his tone is just as flippant, when he claims that it is in the Arts where the true Renaissance can and must be sought. On this subject Vivian waxes very lyrical indeed, looking forward eagerly to the day when the commonplaceness of modern fiction has finally bored everyone to distraction, so that imagination will once again be compelled to take wing;

> And when that day dawns, or sunset reddens, how joyous we shall all be! Facts will be regarded as discreditable, Truth will be found mourning over her fetters, and Romance, with her temper of wonder,

will return to the land. The very aspect of the world will change to our startled eyes. Out of the sea will rise Behemoth and Leviathan, and sail around the high-pooped galleys, as they do on the delightful maps of those ages when books on geography were actually readable. Dragons will wander about the waste places, and the phoenix will soar from her nest of fire into the air. We shall lay our hands upon the basilisk, and see the jewel in the toad's head. Champing his gilded oats, the Hippogriff will stand in our stalls, and over our heads will float the Blue Bird singing of beautiful and impossible things, of things that are lovely and that never happen, of things that are not and that should be.

Hard on the heels of this flight of fancy Vivian lays down, by way of summary, a series of formal doctrines for his new (or renewed) aesthetics. The first is that Art never expresses anything but itself: that it is not a reflective product of its age, but something which evolves and moves according to its own innate whims. The second is that all bad art is inspired by attempts to make art more representative, and that any attempt by an artist to be true to Life or Nature is a mistake. The third restates the dictum that Life (and Nature) imitate Art rather than vice versa. The fourth, the *quod erat demonstrandum* of the exercise, is that Lying—"the telling of beautiful untrue things"—is the proper aim of Art.

These claims are, of course, more modest than those made by Lord Henry Wootton or Des Esseintes who, being Lies themselves, were fully entitled to be more extravagant than the artists who created them. It might be noted, however, that Oscar Wilde made a more strenuous effort to live by his philosophy than Joris-Karl Huysmans ever did; and that his determination to live as a work of art, unfettered by realism of outlook or any particular respect for the dictates of nature, cut tragically short his dazzlingly brilliant career as a Liar par excellence, and landed him in Reading Gaol.

A few brief addenda to Wilde's views on art—which may be taken to reflect his final recorded thoughts upon the matter—can be found in Laurence Housman's book *Echo de Paris* (1923), which recalls a conversation between Wilde, Housman, and two other friends which took place in Paris in the autumn of 1899. Here we find Wilde advising one of his acolytes to learn life only by inexperience, so that it will always be unexpected and delightful; "never realize" is, he suggests, the ideal dictum. We also find him ready to associate the beauty of failure and the nobility of exile, on the grounds that only by tasting utter failure, with or without a leavening of intermediate success, can an artist perceive his own soul—and, within his own soul, the world entire.

These comments are easily read in isolation as a melancholy but superficial comedy, which attempts to make a virtue of disaster by means of the same strategy of casual inversion that marked all Wilde's most famous epigrams, and which matches his temperament so closely to that of Des Esseintes. The notion of the artist perceiving his own soul is, however, twice elaborated and re-emphasized later in the conversation. The first time the issue is raised again is to clear up a misconception. Wilde finds it necessary to insist that he spoke of perception and not of knowledge, and to state frankly that understanding of oneself, or the world, is impossible: that the soul is always a stranger, and a hostile one. He had said much the same thing in what is perhaps the best of his many fantasies, "The Fisherman and his Soul," and he reiterates it yet again here in the second of two brief tales which he volunteers to tell his hearers (because he knows that he will never write them down). This allegorical prose poem explains how a man sells his burdensome soul for its proper price—thirty pieces of silver—but becomes miserable because he is no longer capable of sin; after searching the world in the hope of finding and regaining his soul, he finally buys it back at what is now its proper price—his body—but finds it unutterably foul.

This allegory serves to remind us that Vivian's flight of fancy regarding the rewards of a renaissance of Lying is deliberately optimistic. The power of the imagination does not merely reveal wonders, but also horrors. That clear sight which penetrates the sham of realism finds all manner of chimerical monsters. The true Decadent knows this, and never forgets it. Wilde's aesthetic philosophy embodies this consciousness, but also tries to find a way through it; it has as much in common with the recovered idealism of Mallarmé as the ironic pessimism of Huysmans. The moralistic aspects of Wilde's work are not simply a mask provided to make them more acceptable to the public eye; there is a depth of conviction in them which is sincere in spite of its unease.

* * * * * * *

For a brief period before Wilde's trial the idea of Decadence did become fashionable enough in London to generate its own periodical press, whose flagship was John Lane's quarterly *Yellow Book*, launched in 1894. By far the most famous (or notorious) contributor to the *Yellow Book*, however, was not a writer but an illustrator—the art editor Aubrey Beardsley, who had also designed the binding for Lane's "Keynotes" series, in which several notable Decadent works were featured. It was Beardsley's illustrative work rather than any production in poetry or prose which provided English Decadence with a memorable image. His astonishing decorations for Lord Alfred Douglas's English translation of Wilde's *Salomé* (1894) were far more original, exotic, and daring than any other products of the Movement. The evidence of his incomplete baroque romance *Under the Hill* (1897) suggests that Beardsley might have become a genuine Decadent writer too, but he was given no opportunity to do so because he died of tuberculosis in 1898.

The early issues of the *Yellow Book* did endeavor to provide Beardsley's artwork with some appropriate textual support, but the poetry featured therein was essentially staid and the most interesting item—Max Beerbohm's ironically flippant commentary on the cult of artificiality, "A Defence of Cosmetics"—only proved controversial because some readers did not realize that it was a joke. A similar flippancy was exhibited by a series of *Stories Toto Told Me*, which were contributed by the colorful conman "Baron Corvo" (Frederick W. Rolfe).

Any pretensions to authentic Decadence which the *Yellow Book* may have had were instantly jettisoned in the wake of the Wilde trial, although Wilde had never actually been a contributor. Beardsley was sacked for having (innocently) kept such bad company, and though he was promptly hired by Arthur Symons to work on *The Savoy*, a new periodical which was supposed to take up where the *Yellow Book* left off, the hastily-dropped torch of English Decadence proved too hot to handle. *The Savoy* lasted only eight issues, closing with a December 1896 issue in which all the text was supplied by Symons and all the illustrations by an ailing Beardsley; when it died, the English Decadent Movement, such as it had been, died too.

The body of English work which was produced with the Decadent label actually in mind is understandably thin, given that the term was in vogue for little more than three years, and the work to which the label can be attached at second hand is not much larger. The most intensely lurid products of English Decadence can be found in a small group of short story collections issued between 1893 and 1896: Count Eric Stenbock's *Studies of Death* (1893); R. Murray Gilchrist's *The Stone Dragon and Other Tragic Romances* (1894); and three "Keynotes" volumes: Arthur Machen's *The Great God Pan and the Inmost Light* (1894); and M. P. Shiel's *Prince Zaleski* (1895) and *Shapes in the Fire* (1896). John Lane also produced the book version of Clemence Housman's novella *The Were-Wolf* (1896), which had been first published in the preceding year.

Stenbock, who was by far the most enthusiastic Decadent in London, was not an Englishman by birth, although he had studied at Oxford and wrote in English. Because he was a foreigner, his conspicuous indulgence of the Decadent lifestyle was deemed understandable, if not forgivable. He lived amid absurd decorations, addicted to drink and drugs, and was more flamboyantly homosexual than

Oscar Wilde. His (mostly self-published) poems had long been ignored, and he must have greeted the advent of an English Decadent Movement gladly, hopeful that he might now be "discovered." Alas, although Arthur Symons did condescend to notice Stenbock, he did not shirk from describing him as "inhuman." As it turned out, *Studies of Death* was his last work; he died in 1895.

Gilchrist, Machen, Shiel, and Clemence Housman, by contrast, were writers at the beginning of their careers. As in Stenbock's case, all four are remembered today mainly because their supernatural stories are often reprinted in collections of horror stories, but they all went on to produce work in a markedly less Decadent (and mostly less interesting) vein. Two of the four, however, were marked deeply enough by their flirtation with Decadence that they never quite shook off its legacy. Machen and Shiel both survived until 1947, when they were in their eighties, and although neither of them was subsequently to write anything quite as overwrought as "The Great God Pan" or the stories in *Shapes in the Fire* they carried certain Decadent motifs and stylistic sympathies forward into the twentieth century, and never quite let go of them.

Machen's best novel, *The Hill of Dreams* (written 1897; published 1907), is a story of escape into the past more extreme and more determined than Huysmans's *Là-bas*, and presents a memorable account of splenetic civilization-phobia. Shiel's best novel, *The Purple Cloud* (1901), has the last man alive in the world giving extravagant vent to his anguish amidst the ruins. Machen and Shiel both sought philosophical foundations for their sustained Decadent consciousness, Machen in mysticism and Shiel in a quasi-Nietzschean conviction that the coming of the *übermensch* was vital to a renewal of the cause of progress. Even so, their later work retains an affectation for stylistic ornamentation and an ironic but sincere scepticism regarding the value of contemporary morality (especially in connection with orthodox religion).

The extravagant use of the supernatural which these four authors made was not much different in manner and tone from the uses of the supernatural to be found in the *contes* of Jean Lorrain and Rémy de Gourmont (or, indeed, from the uses made by Théophile Gautier), but they had the advantage of an alternative tradition into which they could readily be relocated. Although the English Gothic novel had faded away with the Romantic Movement, there had grown up in late Victorian times a rich tradition of ghost stories. This tradition had begun with Charles Dickens's moralistic "Christmas books," but its preservation within the Christmas annuals which many English periodicals issued had broadened to include both sentimental fantasies and outright horror stories.

* * * * * *

The translocation of these Decadent works into the still-evolving tradition of British weird fiction was further justified by the fact that the erotic passions which had been so comprehensively excluded from realistic fiction had occasionally found expression—albeit in cryptically encoded form—in works of supernatural fiction. The most erotically intense work produced in Britain during Victoria's reign was Christina Rossetti's "Goblin Market" (1862), whose symbolic analysis of the personal politics of tasting "forbidden fruit" may be more revealing than she intended. In addition to Oscar Wilde, Dublin's Trinity College played temporary host to two Anglo-Irish writers who took up the motif of the vampire which had been deployed as an erotic metaphor by Gautier and Baudelaire. J. Sheridan le Fanu's "Carmilla" (1872) is a very striking representation of perverse eroticism, which Bram Stoker was trying consciously to emulate when he wrote the best-selling *Dracula* (1897).

Another writer who found supernatural fiction a useful medium for the expression of erotic material was Vernon Lee, who was one of several English homosexual writers who went into voluntary exile. Her relatively straightforward novella *A Phantom Lover* (1886) was reprinted in 1890 in *Hauntings* along with two remarkably vivid tales of adamantine *femmes fatales*, "Amour Dure" and "Dionea." Her heavily ironic *Yellow Book* fantasy "Prince Alberic and the Snake Lady" (1896) had to wait until 1907 to be reprinted in *Pope Jacynth and Other Fantastic Tales*, along with several other tales inspired by such French models as Anatole France, while the feverish erotic fantasy "The Virgin of the Seven Daggers" (1889) did not appear in book form until 1927; but it is possible in retrospect to see Lee as one of the prime movers of English Decadence, who would surely have done more work in that vein had it been practicable. The quirky sarcasm of her lighter pieces, which take the form of ornate fables gently overturning conventional morality, echoes the work of Richard Garnett, whose brilliantly decorated and magnificently ironic tales were also written under French influence, but he only produced enough of them to fill a single volume: *The Twilight of the Gods* (1888; expanded from sixteen stories to twenty-eight in 1903).

The decorative aspects of English Decadence, which figure so prominently in the work of Oscar Wilde and Vernon Lee, were gradually de-emphasized as its products were absorbed into the horror genre. The stories which became the most significant exemplars were those spiced with a a kind of revulsion which lent itself readily to the construction of stories which were both macabre and morbid. Machen's "The Great God Pan" extrapolated and displayed this element of revulsion to considerable effect. Machen and Yeats, like many of the French Decadents, were very interested in contemporary occultism. Both were associated, albeit briefly, with the Order of the Golden Dawn, which might be regarded as the nearest English equivalent of Péladan's

Parisian Rosicrucian Order, which was eventually taken over by the lifestyle fantasist who was the most wholehearted of all English Decadents: Aleister Crowley. Unfortunately, Crowley had little aptitude for literary work, and his published works are woefully lacking in stylistic and philosophical sophistication. His activities served mainly to intensify the element of revulsion in horror stories which transformed Decadent sensibilities and Decadent ambitions into a stereotype of misguided evil.

The diversion of English Decadence into the tradition of supernatural fiction succeeded in saving some of its most impressive works from stigmatization, but at considerable cost. In a sense, the relabelling of Decadent fantasies as "horror stories" was a capitulation to the forces of Victorian repression, an acceptance of the moralists' definition. The simple truth is, however, that the moralists did win. On the day after the abandonment of the libel action which Wilde unwisely launched against Queensberry, W. E. Henley's *National Observer* published an unsigned leading article which asserted that:

> There is not a man or woman in the English-speaking world possessed of the treasure of a wholesome mind who is not under a deep debt of gratitude to the Marquess of Queensberry for destroying the High Priest of the Decadents. The obscene imposter, whose prominence has been a social outrage ever since he transferred from Trinity Dublin to Oxford his vices, his follies and his vanities, has been exposed, and that thoroughly at last. But to the exposure there must be legal and social sequels...and of the Decadents, of their hideous conceptions of the meaning of Art, of their worse than Eleusinian mysteries, there must be an absolute end.

In a climate of opinion which licensed and fed upon such vituperations, it is hardly surprising that the Decadent label was instantly abandoned by those who had briefly adopted it, and ardently denied in retrospect by all those who had never made the mistake of admitting to it. Art, whether wrought for art's sake or not, was compelled to make its obeisance before the altar of morality like a reluctant heretic in the shadow of the Inquisition.

Such an acute sense of danger speaks of a more than ordinary fear. It testifies to an awareness of crisis. The English writers of Decadent poetry and fiction refrained from calling the British Empire decadent, and most of them refused to abandon hope for the future, but their enemies, in reacting as if they had, gave the game away. The Empire was in a state of irreversible decline, and what the future promised was not (as jingoistic patriots liked to believe) a war that would end war and secure Anglo-Saxon hegemony for all time. A war there would be, but it turned out to be a great orgy of stupid butchery which would test almost to destruction every optimistic philosophy of progress which could be rallied against its apocalyptic implications, whether religious, political, or technophilic. The crucifixion of Oscar Wilde by the rampant spirit of imperial vanity proved to be the prelude to the crucifixion of an entire generation, sent to die in the muddied fields of northern France.

X.

FIN DE SIECLE:

THE DECADENT HERITAGE

The Decadent Movements of France and England suffered their own decline and fall. Many historians and critics have argued that whatever was valuable within them was claimed and transformed into something finer by the triumphant advance of Symbolism. If this is indeed what happened it may be seen as a full turn of the critical wheel. The kind of apologetic case compiled by Arthur Symons, which insists that the word "decadent" only applies to matters of style and not to matters of morality, is not so very different from the argument constructed by Gautier to introduce *Les Fleurs du mal*. It is a view which retains a certain reluctant sympathy for a Rimbaudian "rational disordering of the senses," but very little for the kind of defiant anguish that possessed men like Lorrain and Mirbeau.

To divorce the Decadent style from its typical subject-matter is effectively to conclude that, although the Decadents had certain interesting mannerisms, they were wrong about the sickness in themselves and wrong about the sickness of the world—wrong not only at the level of diagnosis but at the level of feeling. Such a case is easy enough to make, given that the march of progress has continued to accelerate throughout the last century. The Great War may have put a quasi-apocalyptic end to the Parisian *monde* which the Decadents loved and hated so intensely, but the world, and Paris, went on regardless. Modern medicine tamed the ravages of syphilis and tuberculosis, and modern psychology discarded the worthless theory of hereditary degeneracy.

On the other hand, it certainly cannot be said that feelings of personal existential malaise, and the feeling that civilization itself is somehow sick, have ever been conclusively banished. Such a sense of fundamental unease may be the property of a minority, but it was always that. Nor has that other Decadent bugbear—a naïve Rousseauesque faith in the goodness of Nature—lost its force as a tempting but ultimately fatuous first response to such a sense of unease. Other, more nearly Decadent responses—including the uses of psychotropic drugs to achieve a calculated disordering of the senses—are still relatively commonplace.

It is still possible, in the age of environmental pollution, biological warfare, future shock, and AIDS, to feel something akin to what the Decadents felt and to respond in ways not unlike the the Decadents responded. The Decadent Movement may have suffered its own decline and fall, but the idea that modern society and modern civilization are still locked into an ongoing decline and still under threat of an imminent fall remains. In fact, as we approach the *fin* of yet another *siècle*—this one the end of a millennium too—the feelings which generated the literature of Decadence seem to be growing stronger again. Although there is no evident Decadent Movement in modern literature, it is not difficult to locate and identify the key features of Decadent consciousness within its broad and complicated spectrum.

For this reason, if for no other, it would be inappropriate to end a study of the Decadent Movements of France and England with their apparent disappearance. It might in fact, be more sensible to consider their fate as a temporary eclipse or relative fragmentation rather than a conclusive disappearance, and to examine in more detail the exact manner in which their elements were hidden or broken up.

Stéphane Mallarmé's progress—as perceived by those who viewed his career in retrospect—from Decadence to Symbolism had less to do with his published work than his declarations of intent. He set out to discover that which wholehearted Decadents considered impossible of achievement: a new poetic Ideal and a quasi-religious poetic mission. Although Mallarmé never actually produced the Grand Oeuvre about which he was always talking, it nevertheless sufficed as a hypothetical goal towards which all his work could be retrospectively reorientated. He laid down for his later followers a manifesto for life and art which was less uncomfortable to follow and more attractive as an item of commitment than the Decadent philosophy. (Mallarmé seems, of course, to have been a much happier man than Baudelaire, Rimbaud, Verlaine, Huysmans, Lorrain, or Mirbeau.)

As the proto-psychological theories which had briefly dignified their excesses fell into decline, it is hardly surprising that all but the hardiest of the Decadents deflected their careers into more promising literary territory, mostly accepting Mallarmé's offer of renewed hope and revitalized significance. Nevertheless, the legacy of the French Decadent Movement lingered until the end of one century and into the early years of the new one, and it is instructive to examine the eventual fates of those who were—however briefly—caught up in it.

* * * * * *

By the time Jean Lorrain died in 1906, Joris-Karl Huysmans (who died in 1907) had transformed his Decadent consciousness into religiosity, and Rémy de Gourmont (who died in 1915) had subsumed his within adventures in Grand Theory. Some writers who had seemed likely to make a significant contribution to the movement had died even earlier; others lived long thereafter. Like Huysmans and Gourmont, most of those who survived underwent marked changes of literary direction. The brief "case notes" which follow are blatantly inadequate as supplements to the essays presented in previous chapters, but they will perhaps allow the more detailed case studies to be more precisely located within their wider context.

Jules Laforgue died of tuberculosis in 1887 at the age of twenty-seven. Although his early poetry definitely belongs to the Movement, he was never a wholehearted Decadent; his sense of irony was far too powerful. Like Tristan Corbière—one of Verlaine's *poètes maudits*, who had died in 1875—he contrived to transform a fundamentally gloomy outlook by the power of ironic wit, and his work was already moving in the direction of extraordinarily ornate satire when it was brought to its premature end. His penchant for sparkling wordplay and pyrotechnic sarcasm is shown to best effect in his collection of six prose pieces, *Moralités légendaries* (1887), in which the pretensions of heroes like Perseus, Lohengrin, and Hamlet are mercilessly deflated.

The Comte de Villiers de L'Isle-Adam, who died in 1889, must be regarded as a key influence on the Decadents rather than a part of the Movement. Although his *Contes cruels* (1883) were praised by Des Esseintes in *A rebours* and gave a title to a favorite Decadent subgenre, Villiers's work is marked by an urgent Idealism which kept ennui and impuissance out of his literary agenda. The Decadent aristocrat Lord Ewald, in Villier's misogynistic fantasy *L'Eve future* (1886), finds an extraordinary way to transcend his predicament, when the inventor Edison builds him a perfect woman (thus taking the cult of the artificial to a new extreme); but Villiers went on to develop a conscientiously neo-Romantic extravagance in such visionary dramas as the posthumously-published *Axël* (1890).

Georges Michel, who wrote under the name Ephraïm Mikhaël and died in 1890, was another who had very little time to make his mark upon the world, but he collaborated briefly with Catulle Mendès, and published a number of interesting Decadent prose-poems, one of which—"Solitude"—is an intriguing allegory which echoes Baudelaire in adopting the subtitle, "Anywhere Out of the World." He too showed distinct signs of embracing a new Romanticism, or at least taking refuge in decorous exoticism.

Georges Rodenbach died in 1898, at the age of forty-three. He was one of the central figures in the literary revival of La Jeune Belgique, which borrowed stylistic devices from the Parisian Decadent Movement, but was always so conscious of its own "youthfulness" as to be relentlessly forward-looking. Rodenbach did produce one Decadent classic, however, in *Bruges-la-Morte* (1882), a remarkable exercise in Symbolism in which the hero's obsession with his dead wife effects a visionary transformation of his physical environment, forming a sinister backcloth to his developing fascination with a dancer who is her "double." His later novel *Le Carilloneur* (1897) also features a symbolic Bruges, but here the city's role is very different, pregnant with modernizing forces which the hero regrets, but whose eventual triumph is taken for granted. Oddly enough, he had never lived in Bruges and wrote both books after taking up permanent residence in Paris.

Marcel Schwob died in 1905, at the age of thirty-eight. His first book, *Coeur double* (1891), was a collection of horror stories modelled on Poe and dedicated to Robert Louis Stevenson; he followed it with a book of *contes* whose fantastic content ranges over a much broader spectrum, *Le Roi au masque d'or* (1892), and a volume of prose-poems, *Mimes* (1893). He helped Pierre Louÿs to correct the final draft of Oscar Wilde's *Salomé*, and published a curious fictionalized memoir of his love affair with a terminally-ill prostitute, *Le Livre de Monelle* (1894); he subsequently left the Decadent consciousness behind, striking out in a new direction with his book of imaginary biographies, *Vies imaginaires* (1896).

Catulle Mendès, who died in 1909, was one of the few writers who had built a considerable literary reputation before getting involved with the Decadent Movement (and who spoiled that reputation in the eyes of some later critics by so doing). The novels of his Decadent period are so very typical of their genre—*Zo'har* (1886) is a baroque study of incest; *Méphistophéla* (1890) and *La Maison de la vieille* (1894) offer brutally unsympathetic accounts of Lesbian careers; *La Première maîtresse* (1887) features excursions in which the central characters go hopefully into the Paris slums in search of new sins—that they invite dismissal as exercises in imitation written to cash in on the wave of fashionability, but that would be overly harsh. Mendès always had a Decadent sensibility, which seems to have been awaiting its time; it is displayed to better effect in his short fiction, much of which casts a cynical eye on the game of love. Many of the tales in *Lesbia* (1887) take it for granted that deceit is the lifeblood of romance, and offer pointed examples of calculated insincerity.

Like Jean Lorrain and Anatole France, Mendès also produced fabular *contes* whose morals were carefully subversive of the kind of "civilizing" messages imported into traditional folktales by Perrault and his successors. His one literary masterpiece is an extended exercise in this vein, *Luscignole* (1892), whose final act of ironic cruelty is far more effective in context than the violent deaths which conclude most of his novels of contemporary life.

Pierre Louÿs, who died in 1925, was always on the periphery of the Movement. He was far more interested in the aesthetic glories of Greece than the tarnished grandeur of Rome, but he did translate Lucian's teasing series of dialogues concerning the pragmatic ideology of the courtesan, and he devoted much effort to a quasi-Decadent celebration of Lesbianism in *Les Chansons de Bilitis* (1894). The glorification

127

of Sapphic love is also a significant subtext of his exotic historical novel *Aphrodite* (1896), set in Alexandria during the reign of Cleopatra's elder sister Berenike, which presents a magnificently lurid account of the destructive effect of a grand passion. *La Femme et le pantin* (1898) is another account of humiliation and degradation resulting from irresistible passion, but *Les Aventures de roi Pausole* (1901) is a defiantly light-hearted Rabelaisian exercise in erotomania set in the imaginary realm of Tryphême—which, the author is careful to state, should not be mistaken for Utopia. Unfortunately, Louÿs never completed his next novel, and spent the latter part of his life as a virtual recluse; the causes of his disenchantment and debilitation remain frustratingly unclear.

The most famous of Rodenbach's fellows in the "Young Belgium" movement, Maurice Maeterlinck, died in 1949. He began his career in the late 1880s with poetry of a Decadent stripe, but went on to excel in the field of visionary drama, of a kind which had been pioneered by Villiers de L'Isle-Adam's *Axël*. His early works in this vein feature passive characters who are helpless to defy the frankly mysterious forces which impel them towards their various dooms, but the pessimistic phase, extending from *La Princesse Maleine* (1889) to *La Mort de Tintagiles* (1894), eventually gave way to a much more hopeful one in which the methods of Symbolism are turned to more uplifting and decidedly un-Decadent ends. His most famous work, *L'Oiseau bleu* (1909), is a forceful allegory in which a dreamer's power becomes sufficiently assertive to control and defy the threat of nightmare. Later still he turned to social and psychological realism, but he remains firmly linked with a dilute aesthetic mysticism which might be regarded as a pale but respectable shadow of the kind of lifestyle fantasy which sustained Péladan and briefly tempted Huysmans.

Rachilde, who died in 1953, was of course at the very heart of the Movement from its beginning. She was a frequent contributor to *Le Décadent*, and proudly proclaimed that her childish innocence and mental health had been utterly corrupted by the allure of artifice and neurosis. Her application for an amazon license notwithstanding, however, she maintained a private rectitude which cast doubt on her wholeheartedness if not her sincerity. Her early novels presented a spirited defense of uninhibited eccentricity, offering a series of portraits of forceful Decadent heroines, most of whom are triumphantly unredeemed even by death, but she never made any serious attempt to follow their example. The separation of reality and imagination which she achieved can, however, be viewed as a triumph rather than a hypocrisy; it is arguable that she was the one Decadent whose expeditions "out of the world" were entirely successful, in that their safety was never compromised by their extremism.

Rachilde's heroines are unreal, and she would not associate herself with them even to the extent of claiming to be a feminist, but they nevertheless provided a remarkable series of liberating dream-figures. The androgynous Raoule de Vénérande, heroine of *Monsieur Vénus* (1884), treats her handsome but low-born young lover as a sex-object, and eventually installs his mummified corpse within her boudoir when he is murdered by a rival. The promiscuous and dandified heroine of *Nono* (1885) is prone to murder inconvenient lovers. *La Marquise de Sade* (1887) and *L'Animale* (1893) are elaborate analyses of the growth and eventual flowering of an unorthodox moral consciousness; the bestial analogies of the latter novel are extrapolated into the supernatural in *La Princesse des ténèbres* (1896), whose heroine is infected with lycanthropy by her lover. The heroine of *La Jongleuse* (1900) is emotionally torn between two lovers, one of whom is a Greek vase.

Rachilde made considerable progress in freeing literary representations of female sexuality from the morass of male pornographic fantasy, and her crusade was subsequently taken up by Colette once she had freed herself from exploitative collaboration with her husband Willy. Although she continued to write well into the twentieth century, Rachilde gradually shed the apparatus of her make-believe Decadence. She toned down the sexual *bizarrerie* of her books considerably, and assumed a less celebratory attitude to moral deviance. Her work became increasingly nostalgic and conservative in its values; her later novels are mostly accounts of doomed relationships, in which the eccentric lusts which so excited her in earlier days play an uncompromisingly destructive role. She was, in the end, the only Decadent who lived to be genuinely old, but in so doing she certainly faded away.

Charles Bargone, who died in 1957 and who wrote under the pseudonym Claude Farrère, began his career as a *protégé* of Pierre Louÿs, but came too late upon the scene to be involved in the Movement. He did, however, produce the ultimate study of the Decadent use and abuse of drugs in his remarkable story-cycle *Fumée d'opium* (1904), which followed the example of Jules Boissière's *Les Fumeurs d'opium* (1896) in confusing and blending exotic dream-experiences with exotic Oriental landscapes. Together with *A rebours*, published twenty years earlier, it brackets the field of Decadent narrative prose. Farrère was to go on to produce many works whose upbeat exoticism was similar to that of Pierre Loti. That neo-Romanticism combined with political commitment drew him well away from Decadent consciousness, but it is worth noting that his vivid futuristic fantasy *Les Condamnés à mort* (1920) features a hopeless revolution of the redundant proletariat against Capitalists whose comforts have robbed them of all moral sensibility. Like the other writers touched by the Movement's ideas and ideals, he never entirely lost sight of its basic presumptions about the state and likely fate of the civilized world.

* * * * * * *

The fate of the English Decadent Movement—that is to say, the diversion of its methods and materials into the field of supernatural fiction—can also be seen as a reversion to an earlier phase. Baudelaire developed his Decadent style under the powerful influence of Edgar Allan Poe, whose influence on later writers in America was almost entirely confined to the relatively disreputable field of supernatural fiction, which went into a marked decline once Nathaniel Hawthorne had followed him to the grave in 1864. It is, however, very obvious that when American supernatural fiction took on a new lease of life at the turn of the century, the example of Poe was to some degree compounded with that of the French fiction which had been written under his influence.

There was, of course, no American Decadent Movement. America was the last place on Earth to provide fertile soil for literary Decadence, because it was the nation most thoroughly infected with the mythology of progress and the home of the frontier spirit. In the eyes of every "right-thinking" American, decadence was a purely European problem, to be derided and deplored. Later generations tended to regard Poe as an un-American wimp, and this dismissive attitude, combined with a rigid puritanism which considered almost all French fiction indecent and all pretensions to literary style effete, was a powerful disincentive to would-be experimenters with Decadence.

In spite of these disincentives—or rather in reaction against them—America continually produced rebel "Bohemians" who despised the crassness of their own culture and venerated European sophistication. While the Decadent Movements enjoyed their brief heyday in Paris and London, some American Bohemians did take aboard elements of Decadent consciousness and Decadent style. The early works of Edgar Saltus show such influences, *Mr. Incoul's Misadventure* (1887) hinting at the existence of an occult underworld in New York, and lush historical romances like *Imperial Purple* (1892) taking mock-censorious delight in detailing the decadence of ancient Rome. James Huneker's early short stories, collected in *Melomaniacs* (1902) and *Visionaries* (1905), take a similar delight in exoticism. So narrow were the restrictions under which these writers labored, however, that the erotic elements in their work are very subdued. The bilingual Stuart Merrill, whose anthology of translations of French prose-poems *Pastels in Prose* (1890) provided a useful set of exemplars, wrote all his original works in French. Lafcadio Hearn, whose translations of Gautier provided the models of English Decadent style, found Japan a much more comfortable place to work. It was, however, the displacement of Decadent motifs into supernatural fiction which provided Ambrose Bierce with the extra latitude which he needed, in the more baroque items collected in *Tales of Soldiers and Civilians* (1891) and *Can Such Things Be?* (1893).

One of the items included in Bierce's first collection, "An Inhabitant of Carcosa," impressed Robert W. Chambers, who returned to America after a brief spell as an art student in Paris and published two collections of stories based in his experiences there; it is echoed in a remarkable group of four stories which commenced the second of those collections, *The King in Yellow* (1895). Chambers soon put his Parisian interlude behind him and went on to become a prolific writer of romantic comedies and historical novels imbued with a thoroughly American decorum and sentimentality, but the four supernatural tales about the evil influence of the eponymous play on those unlucky enough to read it made a deep impression on some of their own readers.

Bierce was to influence, directly and indirectly, several other writers who lived—as he did—on the Western seaboard of the U.S.A., including Edward Markham and George Sterling. Sterling found in Bierce one of the few men able to provide an understanding and sympathetic audience for his morbid and highly-decorated work. He was doomed to be esoteric and largely unread while he lived (and to remain so), but he enjoyed a brief moment of celebrity—or notoriety—when Bierce persuaded *Cosmopolitan* to publish his bizarre poetic hymn to escapism, "A Wine of Wizardry" (1907).

Some immigrant writers did their best to initiate the American public into the joys of Decadence. George Sylvester Viereck published volumes of verse and drama in 1906-07, as well as the homoerotic fantasy *The House of the Vampire* (1907), but found it impossible to continue publishing work in that vein. He became a journalist, as did Ben Hecht, whose own determinedly and extravagantly Decadent novella *Fantazius Mallare* (1922) was issued in a limited edition for "private circulation" to "subscribers" because it could not be openly sold, and was prosecuted nevertheless on the grounds that its illustrations were obscene. Viereck did succeed, eventually, in breaching this wall of puritanism, and did so in no uncertain terms when he and Paul Eldridge achieved best-seller status with a sprawling erotic fantasy chronicling the adventures of the Wandering Jew, *My First Two Thousand Years* (1928); but he was following a directional pointer which had long been set, establishing that even mildly Decadent style and mildly Decadent subject-matter had to be displaced into overtly fantastic fiction if they were to be deemed acceptable. James Branch Cabell had done likewise, although it had not saved *Jurgen* (1919) from prosecution on the grounds that its carefully-encoded sexual symbolism was too easily penetrable.

There is, of course, a definite propriety in this kind of displacement, which affected many of the writers at the heart of the French Decadent Movement. The dynamic of their work had always been centrifugal, flying off in all directions from its actual basis, aiming for anywhere out of the world. It is not at all surprising that the most fervent of all Poe's American descendants brought such flights into fantasy to certain logical limits which no French or English writers ever reached.

Ambrose Bierce's *protégé* George Sterling attracted a handful of *protégés* of his own, prominent among them Clark Ashton Smith, who tried to take over where Sterling left off as the poet of American Decadence, translating a good deal of Baudelaire and writing his own imitations thereof before outdoing "A Wine of Wizardry" in his own escapist epic "The Hashish-Eater" (1922). Like Sterling, though, Smith had no hope of finding a wide audience for his work, and he was able to carry his enthusiasm into prose fiction only because of a brief period of freakish fashionability which he enjoyed in the pulp magazine *Weird Tales*, for which he produced what were and still remain the most lushly exotic escapist fantasies ever written.

Smith soon entered into correspondence with the man whose peculiar theories of the aesthetics of horror engulfed many of the writers who appeared in *Weird Tales*, although he was never actually its editor: H. P. Lovecraft. Lovecraft made extravagant, if belated, use of such Decadent tropes as hereditary degeneracy, ultimately formulating a strange cosmic perspective which made such degeneracy a condition of the universe. Although he remained inextricably bound up in American moral puritanism, Lovecraft's aesthetic theories were thoroughly Decadent, and many of his other correspondents, including the poets Samuel Loveman and Vincent Starrett, assiduously turned out Decadent work for which there was no obvious audience at all.

Lovecraft died without ever seeing his own work collected, but the circle which had formed around him proved astonishingly resilient, and its efforts to preserve and disseminate his work and ideas eventually succeeded in establishing him as an enormously influential figure within—and, to an increasing extent, beyond—the field of American weird fiction. Any reader in the modern era whose soul desires to be taken "anywhere out of the world" is as likely to be drawn to the extremism of strangeness represented by the work of Lovecraft and Smith as to the moral and philosophical experiments of those French Decadents who sought more straightforward expression of their anguished sentiments.

* * * * * *

Barbey d'Aurevilly was, of course, wrong to argue that the only possible escape routes for the earnest Decadent were a fervent recommitment to the Catholic faith and an ignominious death. Religious faith is far from the only ideal to which a man might commit himself in order to recover the sense of being and doing something worthwhile; various aesthetic and political creeds offered convenient exits for Decadents disenchanted with disenchantment, and they were used to good advantage. Even those who found it impossible to embrace any faith at all could learn to look at themselves and their work more ironically, becoming self-mocking but essentially self-satisfied satirists. Nor, for that matter, can death be regarded as an end, let alone as an escape, within the framework of the Decadent consciousness. The very essence of the idea of Decadence is that death is merely a passing moment within a continuing process of decay.

It is, therefore, entirely appropriate that echoes of the Decadent consciousness should continue to sound throughout the twentieth century, sometimes at long distances from its point of origin in Paris. Baudelaire's work is more alive now, and much more widely read now, than it ever was before. Although his analyses of spleen and ennui have to be understood—if they are to be understood properly—in their proper historical context, they have nevertheless become immortal in the crystallizations of Decadent sensibility which are provided by *Les Fleurs du mal* and the prose-poems. Baudelaire's particular flowers of evil may not have been hardy perennials, but they have not withered into dust. Obsolete literary fads never really die, nor do they entirely fade away. They live on, undissolved and untransformed, in the organized chaos of potential influences, preserved in memory as treasures to be looted, follies to be satirized, and bad examples to be avoided.

For some time now it has been difficult to take the Decadent pose entirely seriously. Antibiotics have dramatically reduced the horrors of venereal disease, and in so doing have devastated the pattern of symbols, metaphors, and analogies which lies at the heart of *A rebours*. HIV viruses are now beginning to take up some of the imaginative slack left behind by the once-dreaded spirochaetes, but the modern medical context forbids any simple regeneration of the outmoded tropes. Diseases do not threaten us the way they used to, and in becoming less mysterious have become less fascinating. The same sort of thing has happened to perfumery and the creation of new flowers; they have been reduced from the arcane mysteries they once were to mere matters of industrial chemistry and selective breeding. We know now that the world is not as magical as it once seemed; even religious men now find it far more difficult than they did before to believe six impossible things before breakfast, and those who can still do it run a far greater risk of being called crackpots.

Despite Vivian's charmingly vivid hopes, as expressed in "The Decay of Lying," the realistic novel has so far kept the perceived hegemony in the literary world which it won in the late nineteenth century. Romance flourishes alongside it, but its quality is often compromised and undermined by its sheer quantity; the contemporary glut of genre fantasy serves mainly to demonstrate that even the most exotic products of the mythopoeic imagination can be regulated by convention in such a way as to become every bit as tedious, repetitive, colorless, and moralistically simple-minded as the dullest products of representative art.

133

For this reason, the hopes of Wildean aesthetes have become as much of a mockery as their fears.

* * * * * * *

Any summary of the achievements of Decadence must begin by admitting that the foundations of the movement were built on sand. Its central myths were false, and its shocking innovations have lost their shock value in becoming familiar. A sensitive study of history provides little evidence to support the notion that all great civilizations must crumble because the comforts consequent upon success are fatally corrosive of further ambition or effective self-defense. Modern psychology has outgrown the idea that genius is a species of madness, and modern biology has exposed the folly of the notion that bloodlines degenerate with the passage of time. There is nothing particularly startling to the modern mind in the notion of art for art's sake, and there is no longer the least air of mystery surrounding hashish or opium derivatives. Nobody these days talks about a cult of artificiality (although the merest glance at the contemporary genre of "shopping and fucking" best-sellers testifies to the fact that its modern equivalent is more of a religion). A contemporary essay on the defense of cosmetics, however broadly the term might be construed, could only be a conservative reaction against the shocking radicalism of greens and feminists.

One can, of course, make a feeble apologetic case for the Decadent Movements on the grounds that they helped lay the groundwork for subsequent movements like Surrealism and Modernism, and offered some useful exemplars to later writers, but any such apology would be a damnation rather than a salvation. The Decadents certainly did not intend to be a mere passing phase on the way to something more worthwhile; they assumed that they were harbingers of the apocalypse, and they wanted to reach an extreme which could not be surpassed. Had they been able to anticipate the extent of their failure to achieve those extremes which were realized within forty or fifty years of their passing, they would probably have been depressed—but because they were Decadents they were no strangers to depression, and one more impuissant shrug of the shoulders would have been no big deal. Let us, then, in remembering the celebrants of Decadence, try to discover something more appropriate to say than that they added a few extra drops to the great stream of literary history. Let us try to find something which they say directly to modern readers, which modern readers need to hear.

If we do this, we find that there are two elements of the Decadents' gospel which have neither been falsified nor over-familiarized. Both, as might be expected, are denials of things which the people of the 1880s would very much like to have believed, and which the people of the 1990s are still trying to believe. The Decadents were right, and

are right, about two matters—one important and one admittedly trivial—which have not yet been universally conceded, but ought to be.

The important matter about which the Decadents were right is
their opinion of the veneration of Nature. They thought that it was
stupid: it was and it is. While they had to live with the legacy of
Rousseau, we have to live with a growing Ecological Mysticism which
is a lethal pollutant of green politics and the parent of an indiscriminate
hostility to exactly those aspects of technological progress which might
yet save us from the filthy mess which we are making of the world.
There is a widespread popular misconception to the effect that turning
forests into deserts and rivers into sewers is the prerogative of modern
men armed with sophisticated technologies, and that if only technological progress could be reversed all would be well. In the ears of people
who believe such nonsense there is no more euphonious word than
"natural," which has come to be a synonym for "good."

The Decadents treated such ideas with a scorn which they
thoroughly deserve. They recognized that all the triumphs of mankind
are based in artifice, and that the principal condition of the success of
human life is a secure and complete control of nature. The Decadents
would have condemned as shallow fools those critics who find something perverse and unnatural in the notion of taking control of genetic
processes so that we may become true governors of creation, and they
would have been right to do so. The Decadents might have remained
pessimistic about the actual project of deploying sophisticated techniques of genetic engineering in time to save the world from ruin, but
they would have had no doubts about its propriety. If one can speak at
all about a Decadent Ideal World (and one has to admit that there is a
certain paradox in the notion), then that Ideal World would be a world
in which people had total control over all matters of biology, including
their own anatomy, physiology, and physical desires; it is an Ideal
which we can and ought to share, although far too few of us actually
do.

The trivial matter about which the Decadents were right, although this point might arguably be reckoned a mere corollary of the
first, concerns their cynical attitude to matters of sexual morality—and,
indeed, their dismissal of the ambitions of all prescriptive systems of
morality. They were right—but not particularly original—when they
argued that no set of rules could ever succeed in dampening the perverse curiosity of the human mind; they were right, too, to be severely
sceptical as to whether that acknowledged impossibility is to be regretted.

The mythology of ideal romantic love which is peddled in today's world is not much different from that which was peddled in the
1880s, and there are probably no more people who think that actual
contemporary relationships are accurately reflected in that mythology
than there were then; that is not surprising. What is surprising is that

there are probably as many people, or more, who think that the world would be a far better place if the real world were more like the mythological world of romantic fiction. A generous dose of Decadent literature may still be capable of curing victims of that particular delusion, and it is a prescription which ought at least to be tried.

Even the Decadents, it must be confessed, did have a tendency to regret the non-existence of Ideal Love, but their sense of tragedy was outside the common rut. They shed their fair share of tears over the fact that real people have to make do with lesser affections, which must of necessity be granted to relatively undeserving recipients. But they were also prepared to take an experimental attitude to the problem by suggesting that if the mythology turned out to be an abject failure (as it inevitably would), perhaps it might be stretched and twisted into a better shape by trial and error.

The quest for new sensations—which, inevitably, can also be seen as a search for new sins—was sometimes seen even by the Decadents themselves as little more than an elaborate process of self-destruction, but its underlying attitude of combative derision towards received mythology is perfectly healthy. We live, alas, in a world which is still obsessed with the project of finding and maintaining the perfect relationship, and where a substantial fraction of the periodical press—ads and all—is devoted to an extraordinary elaboration of the typical concerns of "agony columns." The Decadents can tell us, as they told their own contemporaries, that all the advice about how to build the ideal relationship is not only folly but unnecessary folly. Decadents admit that the way the cards are stacked, everyone's life is likely to be a long catalogue of mistakes—but they point out that one doesn't actually have to keep making the same mistakes over and over and over again.

It is mainly because the Decadents say these things, which still need to be said, that there is still some point in reading them. Their stylistic coquetry is not empty even when its illusions have been stripped away; their calculated indecency still poses a real challenge. They can still be alarming and surprising, and even their constant flirtation with certain ideas fit only for the dustbin (which they were unfortunate enough to inherit from incompetent intellectuals) still has a certain redeeming quaintness. Stricken they might have been by ennui, spleen, and impuissance, but when the time came for a Big Push they were never afraid—in spite of their debilitating neurasthenia, cynical wit, and calculated charm—to go over the top and charge headlong into the barbed wire.

* * * * * * *

In view of all this, we surely ought to recognize that time and progress have not eroded everything which the Decadents aspired to do; their black humor remains as clever and mordant as ever, but far too many modern commentators on the Decadent Movements are prone to forget that their leading figures were, after all, comedians. There are as many people today who make the mistake of thinking that Huysmans meant exactly what he wrote as make the same mistake (with slightly more excuse) in respect of Jane Austen; sarcasm is invisible to those who have fully realized the importance of being earnest.

In view of the unfortunate dereliction into which Decadent ideals have fallen, it may be worth restating those Decadent ideas which can bear restating, and which may need restating now more than they needed to be stated then.

Firstly, there is not the slightest reason why art should be restricted and contained by narrow realism, or why realistic representation should be considered one whit more worthy than the wildest fantasy. Magic is useless to engineers but it is invaluable to dreamers, and no man was ever born who was not a dreamer as well as an engineer. Authentically imaginative artists are among the most valuable men alive, and their products should be treasured. It does not matter overmuch exactly where they elect to take us, so long as it is somewhere out of the world.

Secondly, it is absurd and stupid to admire and idolize "Nature" when anyone with an atom of intelligence can see that what we carelessly call "human nature" is all artifice. Nature is neither balanced nor bountiful, despite what certain myths ask us to believe; it is cruel and chaotic. The wise man is one who can recognize artifice for what it is, and put a proper value upon it. The cult of artificiality is the only honest cult there has ever been; while all the rest peddle fatuous deceptions as esoteric truths, the cult of artificiality laments the decay of authentic lies.

Thirdly, we desperately need and ought most ardently to desire a literature of moral challenge, which will fiercely oppose, stoutly defy, and hopefully cure the disease of moral absolutism in whatever form it manifests itself. The greatest tragedy in human history—which is still ongoing—has been the hijacking of moral philosophy by religious dogma, and if there is one thing that everyone in the world ought to pray for it is the annihilation of religion. Whenever anyone proclaims that an item of faith should be deemed "sacred" (which means, of course, immune to rational criticism), it is the duty of all honest men to attack it with every means that art and reason can provide, to see how it stands up to being rubbed the wrong way.

Fourthly, we should be prepared to search out and confront all the petty perversities which lurk inside us, even though we may not ever understand or overcome them. They are, after all, our most intimate selves, far more worthy of being deemed out true selves than the careful masks which we offer to the world in our flatteries, our excuses, our rationalizations, and our poses.

NOTES

CHAPTER II

[1]Gautier, Théophile. *Charles Baudelaire: His Life*, translated by Guy Thorne. New York: Brentano's, 1915, p. 19-20.
[2]Poe, Edgar Allan. "The Murders in the Rue Morgue."
[3]Baudelaire, Charles. "An Invitation to the Voyage," in *The Second Dedalus Book of Decadence (The Black Feast)*, edited by Brian Stableford. Sawtry: Dedalus, 1992, p. 33.
[4]Baudelaire, Charles. "The Double Room," in *The Dedalus Book of Decadence (Moral Ruins)*, edited by Brian Stableford. Sawtry: Dedalus, 1990, p. 121-123.
[5]Baudelaire, Charles. "The Temptations: Eros, Plutus and Fame," in *The Second Dedalus Book of Decadence (The Black Feast)*, edited by Brian Stableford. Sawtry: Dedalus, 1992, p. 314-315.

CHAPTER III

[1]Verlaine, Paul. "Languor," in *The Dedalus Book of Decadence*, edited by Brian Stableford. Sawtry: Dedalus, 1990, p. 95.

CHAPTER V

[1]Huysmans, Joris-Karl. "Des Esseintes' Dream (from *A rebours*)," in *The Second Dedalus Book of Decadence*, edited by Brian Stableford. Sawtry: Dedalus, 1992, p. 41-42.
[2]*Ibid.*, p. 46-47.
[3]Gautier, Théophile. "Hashish," in *Hashish Wine Opium*, by Théophile Gautier and Charles Baudelaire, translated by Maurice Stang. London: Calder & Boyars, 1972, p. 58-60.
[4]Baudelaire, Charles. "Wine and Hashish," in *Ibid.*, p. 85-86.
[5]*Ibid.*, p. 88.

CHAPTER VII

[1]Gourmont, Rémy de. "Stéphane Mallarmé and the Idea of Decadence," in *Decadence and Other Essays on the Culture of Ideas*, translated by William Aspinall Bradley. New York: Harcourt, Brace, 1921, p. 154-55.
[2]Gourmont, Rémy de. *The Natural Philosophy of Love*, translated by Ezra Pound. New York: Boni and Liveright, 1922, p. 150.
[3]Gourmont, Rémy de. *A Virgin Heart*, translated by Aldous Huxley. New York: Modern Library, 1925, p. 160-61.

⁴Gourmont, Rémy de. *Rémy de Gourmont: Selections from All His Works*, chosen and translated by Richard Aldington. New York: Covici-Friede, 1929, p. 346.
⁵*Ibid.*, p. 422-23.
⁶*Ibid.*, p. 361-62.

CHAPTER VIII

¹Mirbeau, Octave. *Torture Garden*, translated by Alvah C. Bessie. New York: Claude Kendall, 1931, p. 258-59.

CHAPTER IX

¹Symons, Arthur. *The Symbolist Movement in Literature*. Rev. ed. London: Constable, 1908, p. 6-7.

SELECTED BIBLIOGRAPHY

PRIMARY SOURCES

Baudelaire, Charles. *Les Fleurs du mal.* Paris: Poulet-Malassis, 1857; translated by Richard Howard as *Les Fleurs du mal.* London: Harvester Press, 1982.

Baudelaire, Charles. *Oeuvres complètes.* Paris: Lévy, 1868-73, 7 vols.; extended ed. Paris: Conard, 1923-65, in 19 vols.

Baudelaire, Charles. *The Poems in Prose, with La Fanfarlo,* translated by Francis Scarfe. London: Anvil Press, 1989.

Bierce, Ambrose. *Tales of Soldiers and Civilians.* San Francisco: Steele, 1891.

Bierce, Ambrose. *Can Such Things Be?* New York: Cassell, 1893.

Chambers, Robert W. *The King in Yellow.* New York: Neely, 1895.

Flaubert, Gustave. *Oeuvres complètes.* Paris: Conard, 1910-54.

Flaubert, Gustave. *La Tentation de Saint Antoine.* Paris: Charpentier, 1874; translated by D. F. Hannigan as *The Temptation of St. Anthony.* London: Nichols, 1895. Earlier version, *La Première tentation de Saint Antoine.* Paris: Charpentier, 1908; translated by René Francis as *The First Temptation of Saint Anthony.* London: Duckworth, 1910.

France, Anatole. *Le Puits de Sainte Claire.* Paris: Calmann-Lévy, 1895; translated by Alfred Allinson as *The Well of Saint Clare.* London: John Lane, 1909.

France, Anatole. *La Révolte des anges.* Paris: Calmann-Lévy, 1914; translated by Winifred Jackson as *The Revolt of the Angels.* London: John Lane, 1914.

Gautier, Théophile. *Oeuvres complètes.* Paris: Lévy, 1855-74, 22 vols.; translated by F. C. de Sumichrast as *Complete Works.* Boston: Brainard, 1900, 12 vols.

Gautier, Théophile. *One of Cleopatra's Nights and Other Stories,* translated by Lafcadio Hearn. New York: Worthington, 1882.

Gilchrist, R. Murray. *The Stone Dragon and Other Tragic Romances.* London: Methuen, 1894.

Gourmont, Rémy de. *Un Coeur virginal.* Paris: Mercure de France, 1907; translated by Aldous Huxley as *A Virgin Heart.* New York: N. L. Brown, 1921.

Gourmont, Rémy de. *Lilith.* Paris: Presses des Essais d'art libre, 1892.

Gourmont, Rémy de. *Le Fantôme.* Paris: Mercure de France, 1893; translated by Francis Amery as "The Phantom" in *The Angels of Perversity.* Sawtry: Dedalus, 1992.

Gourmont, Rémy de. *Les Histoires magiques.* Paris: Mercure de France, 1894; translated by Francis Amery as "Studies in Fascination" in *The Angels of Perversity.* Sawtry: Dedalus, 1992.

Gourmont, Rémy de. *Lettres d'un satyre*. Paris: Crès, 1913; translated by John Howard as *Mr. Antiphilos, Satyr*. New York: Lieber & Lewis, 1922.

Gourmont, Rémy de. *Une Nuit au Luxembourg*. Paris: Mercure de France, 1909; translated by Arthur Ransome as *A Night in the Luxemburg*. London: Swift, 1912.

Gourmont, Rémy de. *D'un pays lointain*. Paris: Mercure de France, 1898.

Gourmont, Rémy de. *Physique de l'amour*. Paris: Mercure de France, 1903; translated by Ezra Pound as *The Natural Philosophy of Love*. New York: Boni & Liveright, 1922.

Hecht, Ben. *Fantazius Mallaré*. Chicago: Covici-McGee, 1922.

Huysmans, Joris-Karl. *A rebours*. Paris: Charpentier, 1884; translated by John Howard as *Against the Grain*. Lieber & Lewis, 1922. Translated by Robert Baldick as *Against Nature*. Harmondsworth: Penguin, 1959.

Huysmans, Joris-Karl. *Là-bas*. Paris: Tresse et Stock, 1891; translated by Keene Wallce as *Down There: Là-bas*. Paris: privately printed, 1928.

Lorrain, Jean. *Buveurs d'âmes*. Paris: Charpentier, 1893.

Lorrain, Jean. *Coins du Byzance; Le Vice errant*. Paris: Ollendorff, 1902.

Lorrain, Jean. *Histoires de masques*. Paris: Ollendorff, 1900.

Lorrain, Jean. *Monsieur de Phocas; Astarté*. Paris: Ollendorff, 1901; translated by Francis Amery as *Monsieur de Phocas*. Sawtry: Dedalus, 1994.

Lorrain, Jean. *Princesses d'ivoire et d'ivresse*. Paris: Ollendorff, 1902.

Louÿs, Pierre. *Aphrodite; Moeurs antiques*. Paris: Mercure de France, 1896; translated by Stanley Reynolds as *Aphrodite*. Paris: Borel, 1900.

Louÿs, Pierre. *Les Aventures de roi Pausole*. Paris: Charpentier, 1901; translated by Mitchell S. Buck as *The Adventures of King Pausole*. New York: The Pierre Louÿs Society, 1926.

Louÿs, Pierre. *Les Chansons de Bilitis*. Paris: Librairie de l'art indépendant, 1895; translated by Horace Manchester Brown as *The Songs of Bilitis*. New York: Aldus Society, 1904.

Machen, Arthur. *The Great God Pan and The Inmost Light*. London: John Lane, 1894.

Mendès, Catulle. *Luscignole*. Paris: Dentu, 1892; translated by Phyllis Mégroz in *Number 56 and Other Stories*. London: T. Werner Laurie, 1928.

Mendès, Catulle. *La Maison de la vieille*. Paris: Charpentier, 1894.

Mendès, Catulle. *La Première maîtresse*. Paris: Charpentier, 1887.

Mendès, Catulle. *Zo'har*. Paris: Charpentier, 1896.

Merrill, Stuart (editor and translator). *Pastels in Prose*. New York: Harper & Bros., 1890.

Mikhaël, Ephraïm. *Oeuvres*. Paris: Lemerre, 1890.

Mirbeau, Octave. *Le Jardin des supplices*. Paris: Charpentier, 1899; translated by Alvah C. Bessie as *Torture Garden*. New York: Claude Kendall, 1931.

Mirbeau, Octave. *Le Journal d'une femme de chambre*. Paris: Charpentier, 1900; translated as *Diary of a Chambermaid*. New York: Didier, 1946.

Mirbeau, Octave. *Les Vingt-et-un jours d'un neurasthénique*. Paris: Charpentier, 1901.

Nerval, Gérard de. *Les Filles de feu*. Paris: Giraud, 1854.

Nerval, Gérard de. *Oeuvres complètes*. Paris: Lévy, 1868-77, 6 vols.

Nerval, Gérard de. *Selected Writings*, translated by Geoffrey Wagner. London: Peter Owen, 1958.

Rachilde. *Contes et nouvelles, suivis du Théâtre*. Paris: Mercure de France, 1900.

Rachilde. *La Jongleuse*. Paris: Mercure de France, 1900; translated by Melanie C. Hawthorne as *The Juggler*. New Brunswick: Rutgers University Press, 1990.

Rachilde. *La Marquise de Sade*. Paris: Monnier, 1887; translated by Liz Heron as *The Marquise de Sade*. Sawtry: Dedalus: 1994.

Rachilde. *Monsieur Vénus*. Bruxelles: Brancart, 1884; translated by Madeleine Boyd. New York: Covici-Friede, 1929.

Rachilde. *Nono, roman de moeurs contemporains*. Paris: Monnier, 1885.

Rachilde. *La Princesse des ténèbres*. Paris: Calmann-Lévy, 1895.

Rimbaud, Arthur. *Oeuvres*. Paris: Mercure de France, 1898.

Rimbaud, Arthur. *Rimbaud*, edited and translated by Oliver Bernard. Harmondsworth: Penguin, 1962.

Rodenbach, Georges. *Bruges-la-Morte*. Paris: Marpon & Flammarion, 1892; translated by Philip Mosley. Paisley: Wilfion Books, 1986.

Schwob, Marcel. *Coeur double*. Paris: Ollendorff, 1891.

Schwob, Marcel. *The King in the Golden Mask and Other Stories*, edited and translated by Iain White. Manchester: Carcanet, 1982.

Schwob, Marcel. *Le Livre de Monelle*. Paris: Chailley, 1894; translated by William Brown Meloney V as *The Book of Monelle*. Indianapolis: Bobbs-Merrill, 1929.

Schwob, Marcel. *Le Roi au masque d'or*. Paris: Olendorff, 1893.

Shiel, M. P. *Prince Zaleski*. London: John Lane, 1895.

Shiel, M. P. *Shapes in the Fire*. London: John Lane, 1896.

Stenbock, Eric. *Studies of Death*. London: Nutt, 1894.

Verlaine, Paul. *Oeuvres complètes*. Paris: Vanier, 1899-1903, 6 vols.

Verlaine, Paul. *Poems by Paul Verlaine*, translated by Gertrude Hall. Chicago: Stone & Kimball, 1895.

Verlaine, Paul. *Hashish and Incense*, translated by François Pirou. New York: The Paul Verlaine Society, 1929.

Viereck, George Sylvester. *The House of the Vampire*. New York: Moffat Yard, 1907.

Villiers de L'Isle-Adam, Comte de. *Axël*. Paris, Quantion, 1890.

Villiers de L'Isle-Adam, Comte de. *Contes cruels*. Paris: Calmann-Lévy, 1883; translated by Hamish Miles as *Sardonic Tales*. New York: Knopf, 1927.

Villiers de L'Isle-Adam, Comte de. *L'Eve future*. Paris: Brunhoff, 1886; translated by Robert Martin Adams as *The Future Eve*. Chicago: University of Illinois Press, 1982.

Wilde, Oscar. *A House of Pomegranates*. London: Osgood McIlvaine, 1891.

Wilde, Oscar. *The Picture of Dorian Gray*. London: Ward, Lock, 1891.

Wilde, Oscar. *Salomé: drame en une acte*. Paris: Librairie de l'art indépendant, 1893; translated by Lord Alfred Douglas as *Salome*. London: E. Mathews & John Lane, 1894.

SECONDARY SOURCES

Birkett, Jennifer. *The Sins of the Fathers: Decadence in France, 1870-1914*. London: Quartet, 1986.

Bourget, Paul. *Essais de psychologie contemporaine*. Paris: Lemerre, 1883; extended ed. in 2 vols., 1889.

Carter, A. E. *The Idea of Decadence in French Literature, 1830-1900*. Toronto: University of Toronto Press, 1958.

Gautier, Théophile. *Charles Baudelaire: His Life*, translated by Guy Thorne. New York: Brentano's, 1915.

Gourmont, Rémy de. *Decadence and Other Essays on the Culture of Ideas*, translated by William Aspinall Bradley. New York: Harcourt, Brace, 1921.

Gourmont, Rémy de. *Selected Writings*, edited and translated by Glenn S. Burne. Ann Arbor: University of Michigan Press, 1966.

Gourmont, Rémy de. *Remy de Gourmont: Selections from All His Works*, translated by Richard Aldington. New York: Covici-Friede, 1929, 2 vols.

Pierrot, Jean. *The Decadent Imagination, 1880-1900*, translated by Derek Colman. Chicago: University of Chicago Press, 1981.

Quennell, Peter. *Baudelaire and the Symbolists*. London: Chatto & Windus, 1929.

Stableford, Brian. *The Dedalus Book of Decadence (Moral Ruins)*. Sawtry: Dedalus, 1990.

Stableford, Brian. *The Second Dedalus Book of Decadence (The Black Feast)*. Sawtry: Dedalus, 1992.

Symons, Arthur. *The Symbolist Movement in Literature* (revised edition). London: Constable, 1908.

Thornton, R. K. R. *The Decadent Dilemma*. London: Edward Arnold, 1983.

Verlaine, Paul. *Les Poètes maudits*. Paris: Vanier, 1884; extended ed., 1888.

Wilson, Edmund. *Axel's Castle*. New York: Charles Scribner's Sons, 1931.

INDEX

Les 120 journées de Sodome (Sade), 9
La 628-E8 (Mirbeau), 106
"A celle qui est trop gaie" (Baudelaire), 16-17
A rebours (Huysmans), 35, 40-49, 52, 54-56, 58, 71, 75, 77-80, 84, 88, 104-105, 107, 112-115, 126, 129, 133
L'Abbé Jules (Mirbeau), 98, 101
"The Absinthe-Drinker" (Symons), 110
Abyssinia, 39
Académie de Dijon (France), 8
Académie Française, 17-18
Affirmations (Huysmans), 111
Against the Grain (Huysmans)—SEE: A rebours
L'Agonie (Lombard), 34
AIDS, 58
L'Aiglon (Rostand), 72
"Amour Dure" (Lee), 121
L'An 2440 (Mercier), 8
ancien régime (France), 8-9
L'Animale (Rachilde), 129
Anti-Jacobin (magazine), 109
Antinoüs, 78
"Anywhere Out of the World" (Baudelaire), 25, 126
Aphrodite (Louÿs), 34, 75, 128
"L'Apparition" (Moreau : painting), 37
L'Après-midi d'un faune (Mallarmé), 35
"Arria Marcella" (Gautier), 19
Astarte (Phoenician goddess), 70, 81-82
Athena (Greek goddess), 36
Augustus, Roman Emperor, 7
Aupick, Jacques, Captain, 16-17
Aurélia (Nerval), 33
Austen, Jane, 137
Auteuil, Paris, France, 74

Les Aventures de roi Pausole (Louÿs), 128
Axël (Villiers de L'Isle-Adam), 126, 128
Baju, Anatole, 40
Balzac, Honoré de, 108
Banville, Théodore de, 18, 38
Barbey d'Aurevilly, Jules-Amédée, 18, 25, 42, 45, 52, 64, 70, 76, 100, 132-133
Barbier, Auguste, 19-22
Bargone, Charles—SEE: Farrère, Claude
Barney, Natalie, 89
Barry, W. F., Rev., 108
Baudelaire, Charles, 13-26, 30-40, 42, 45, 48, 50, 52, 55, 60-61, 64-65, 72-73, 76-77, 85, 90, 96, 104-105, 107, 110-112, 121, 124-126, 130, 132-133
Beardsley, Aubrey, 118
Beckford, William, 11-12
Beerbohm, Max, 119
Bernhardt, Sarah, 72, 74
Bertrand, Aloysius, 18, 21-23
Bibliothèque Nationale (Paris, France), 85-86, 89
Bierce, Ambrose, 130-132
"Les Bijoux" (Baudelaire), 16
Birkett, Jennifer, 112
Blake, William, 12-13
Bois, Jules, 51
Boissière, Jules, 129
The Book of Masks (Gourmont)—SEE: Le Livre des masques
Boullan, Joseph-Antoine, 51
Bourges, Elémir, 41, 71
Bourget, Paul, 64-66, 90
"The Bridge of Sighs" (Hood), 25
Bruges-la-Morte (Rodenbach), 126-127
Brummell, Beau, 70
Brussels, Belgium, 16, 38

Buet, Charles, 42, 70-71
Burne-Jones, Edward, 69
Buveurs d'âmes (Lorrain), 73
Byron, Lord, 12
Byzance (Lombard), 34
Cabell, James Branch, 131
Caligula, Roman Emperor, 7
Le Calvaire (Mirbeau), 100-101
Can Such Things Be? (Bierce), 130
Candide (Voltaire), 99
Le Carilloneur (Rodenbach), 127
"Carmilla" (Le Fanu), 121
Carter, A. E., 112
The Castle of Otranto (Walpole), 11
La Cathédrale (Huysmans), 46, 52
Catholicism, 18, 21, 30, 39, 45, 52, 92, 132
Chambers, Robert W., 131
"La Chambre double" (Baudelaire), 24-25
Les Chansons de Bilitis (Louÿs), 127-128
Les Chants de Maldoror (Lautréamont), 33
Charenton-le-Pont, France, 10
Chartres, France, 52
Le Chat noir (magazine), 39-40, 71
Le Chat Noir Café (Paris, France), 40, 70
Le Chemin de velours (Gourmont), 88, 95
Les Chevaux de Diomède (Gourmont), 89, 94
Christianity, 7, 13, 45, 92-93, 95
"Christmas Books" series (Dickens), 120
"Clarimonde" (Gautier)—SEE: "La Morte amoureuse"
classicism, 37
Cleland, John, 106
Cleopatra, Egyptian Queen, 20, 128
Le Club de Hachischins (France), 17, 59
Coeur double (Schwob), 127
Un Coeur virginal (Gourmont), 89, 93-94
Coleridge, Samuel Taylor, 12, 65
Colette, 75-76, 129
Les Condamnés à mort (Farrère), 129

Condorcet, Marquis de, 8-9, 27
Confessions of an English Opium-Eater (De Quincey), 61
Considérations sur les causes de la grandeur des Romains et des leurs décadents (Montesquieu), 6-7
Constant, Alphonse Louis—SEE: Lévi, Eliphas
contes cruels, 28, 45, 48, 80, 86, 94, 100, 106, 126
Contes cruels (Villiers de L'Isle-Adam), 126
Corbière, Tristan, 126
Corvo, Baron, 119
Cosmopolitan (magazine), 131
Couleurs (Gourmont), 89-90
Courrier français (magazine), 71, 73
Courrière, Berthe, 51, 85, 94
Crane, Walter, 69
Le Crépuscule des dieux (Bourges), 41, 71
Crowley, Aleister, 122
La Culture des idées (Gourmont), 90
"The Cultured Faun" (Johnson), 109
"Danaette" (Gourmont), 87
"The Dance of Salomé" (Moreau : painting), 37, 48, 70
Darwin, Charles, 62
Daubrun, Marie, 17
Daudet, Alphonse, 108
Davidson, John, 109, 111
Days and Nights (Symons), 110
De l'esprit des lois (Montesquieu), 8
De Quincey, Thomas, 61, 65
Le Décadent (magazine), 40, 128
"The Decadent Movement in Literature" (Symons), 109
"The Decay of Lying" (Wilde), 115-117, 133-134
The Decline and Fall of the Roman Empire (Gibbon), 7
"A Defence of Cosmetics" (Beerbohm), 119
Defence of Poetry (Shelley), 12-13
Defoe, Daniel, 106
Delville, Jean, 37
Demeny, Paul, 38
Un Démoniaque (Lorrain), 77
Descartes, René, 11

Le Deuxième livre des masques (Gourmont), 96

Les Diaboliques (Barbey d'Aure-villy), 100

Diary of a Chambermaid (film : 1946), 106

Dickens, Charles, 120

Diderot, Denis, 102

Dingo (Mirbeau), 106-107

"Dionea" (Lee), 121

Divagations (Mallarmé), 36

Dominicans, 68

Douglas, Alfred, Lord, 119

Dowson, Ernest, 109-110

Dracula (Stoker), 121

Le Drageoir aux épices (Huys-mans), 42

Le Dragon impérial (Judith Gau-tier), 104

Dreyfus, Alfred, 74, 98, 101

Du contrat social (Rousseau), 9

"Du vin et du hashish" (Baude-laire), 60-61

Ducasse, Isidore—SEE: Lautré-amont, Comte de

D'un pays lointain (Gourmont), 89

Duval, Amable, 68-69, 72

Duval, Jeanne, 17

Duval, Paul Alexandre Martin—SEE: Lorrain, Jean

Écho de Paris (Housman), 117

Écho de Paris (newspaper), 74

Edel (Bourget), 64

Edison, Thomas A., 100-101, 126

Elba (island), Italy, 10

Eldridge, Paul, 131

Ellen (Lorrain), 72

Ellis, Havelock, 111

Émile (Rousseau), 9

En route (Huysmans), 46, 52

Encyclopédie, ou Dictionnaire raisonné des sciences, des arts et des métiers, 8

Enlightenment, 7, 11-13

Ensor, James, 37, 78

Entartung (Nordau), 65

Esquisse d'un tableau historique du progrès de l'esprit humain (Condorcet), 9

Essais de psychologie contempo-raine (Bourget), 64

L'Eve future (Villiers de L'Isle-Adam), 100, 126

L'Évenement (magazine), 73-74

Exposition Universelle, 75

Eymery, Marguerite—SEE: Rach-ilde

Fabre, J. H., 93

La Fanfarlo (Baudelaire), 30

Fanny Hill (Cleland)—SEE: *Mem-oirs of a Woman of Pleasure*

Fantazius Mallare (Hecht), 131

Le Fantôme (Gourmont), 85, 87, 91-94

Farrère, Claude, 110, 129

Fécamp, France, 69

La Femme et le pantin (Louÿs), 128

"Femmes damnées" (Baudelaire), 16

femmes fatales, 19-20, 34, 37, 70, 74, 79, 100, 121

Les Filles du feu (Nerval), 34

fin de siècle, 36, 56, 75, 77, 95, 125

"The Fisherman and His Soul" (Wilde), 118

Flaubert, Gustave, 17, 34-35, 37, 70

Flecker, James Elroy, 111

Les Fleurs du mal (Baudelaire), 13, 16, 18, 21, 23, 34, 36-37, 52, 73, 105, 107, 124, 133

La Forêt bleue (Lorrain), 70

Fortunio (Gautier), 20

France, Anatole, 34, 45, 80, 95, 97-99, 101, 103, 107, 121, 127

La France (newspaper), 100

Franco-Prussian War (1870), 98, 100

"The French Decadence" (Barry), 108

French Revolution, 9-10

Freud, Sigmund, 87, 111

Fumée d'opium (Farrère), 129

Les Fumeurs d'opium (Boissière), 129

Gandara, Antonio de la, 74

Garnett, Richard, 121

Gaspard de la nuit (Bertrand), 18, 21-23

Gauguin, Paul, 100

Le Gaulois (newspaper), 100

Gautier, Judith, 37, 69, 72, 74, 104

Gautier, Théophile, 14-22, 26, 33, 36-37, 45, 59-61, 73, 89, 91, 104, 110, 120-121, 124, 130
Un Gentilhomme (Mirbeau), 106
Germinal (Zola), 99
Gibbon, Edward, 7, 108
Gide, André, 73
Gilchrist, R. Murray, 119
"Goblin Market" (C. Rossetti), 121
The Golden Journey to Samarkand (Flecker), 111
Goncourt, Edmond, 42, 63-64, 69, 71
Goncourt, Jules, 71
gothic revival, 22-23
Gourmont, Rémy de, 70, 75, 84-96, 98, 100, 112, 120, 125-126
Goya, Francisco, 78
"The Great God Pan" (Machen), 120-121
The Great God Pan and the Inmost Light (Machen), 119
Greek art, 15
Greeks, 7
Les Griseries (Lorrain), 71
Grisi, Carlotta, 19-20, 91
Grisi, Ernesta, 19, 91
Guilbert, Yvette, 74
Hadrian, Roman emperor, 78
Harper's New Monthly Magazine, 109
"Hashish" (Gautier), 59-60
Hashish and Mental Alienation (Moreau), 59
"The Hashish-Eater" (Smith), 132
Hauntings (Lee), 121
Hawthorne, Nathaniel, 130
Hearn, Lafcadio, 130
Hecht, Ben, 131
Helen of Troy, 70
Heliogabalus, Roman Emperor, 7
Henley, W. E., 109, 122
Hernani (Hugo), 19
Hérodiade (Mallarmé), 35
"Hérodias" (Flaubert), 35
The Hill of Dreams (Machen), 120
L'Histoire de Juliette (Sade), 9, 102, 106
Histoire de romanticisme (Gautier), 19
Histoire de[s] masques (Lorrain), 73

Les Histoires magiques (Gourmont), 86-87, 89, 91-92, 94
Hoffmann, E. T. A., 73
homosexuality, 71-73, 79, 121
Hood, Thomas, 25
Horace, 45
The House of the Vampire (Viereck), 131
Housman, Clemence, 119-120
Housman, Laurence, 117
Hugo, Victor, 19-22
Huneker, James, 130
Huysmans, Joris-Karl, 35, 41-56, 58, 60, 71, 74-80, 84-86, 88, 104-105, 107, 109, 111-115, 117, 120, 125-126, 128-129, 133, 137
Hydropathes (French literary group), 70
Iambes (Barbier), 20-21
Ibsen, Henrik, 65
The Idea of Decadence in French Literature, 1830-1900 (Carter), 112
Il pianto (Barbier), 21
L'Île des pingouins (France), 101
Illuminations (Rimbaud), 39
Imperial Purple (Saltus), 130
impressionism, 100, 109
India, 17
Industrial Revolution, 12
"An Inhabitant of Carcosa" (Bierce), 131
The Interpretation of Dreams (Freud), 87
"L'Invitation au voyage" (Baudelaire), 24
Iskender (Judith Gautier), 104
Italy, 21
Izambard, Georges, 38
Jacquemin, Jeanne, 74-76
Le Jardin des supplices (Mirbeau), 97, 99-107
Jarry, Alfred, 75, 86
Jesuits, 98-99, 101
La Jeune Belgique (Belgian literary movement), 126, 128
Joan of Arc, 50-51
Johnson, Lionel, 109-110
La Jongleuse (Rachilde), 129
Joséphine, French Empress, 10
"Le Joujou-patriotisme" (Gourmont), 86
Le Journal (newspaper), 74-76

Le Journal d'une femme de chambre (Mirbeau), 106
Juin, Hubert, 68
Jurgen (Cabell), 131
Justine, ou les malheurs de vertu (Sade), 9, 33, 106
Kant, Immanuel, 95
"Keynotes" publishing series (John Lane), 118
Khnopff, Fernand, 37
The King in Yellow (Chambers), 131
Kropotkin, Pëtr, 99
Là-bas (Huysmans), 45, 50-52, 74, 85, 120
Laforgue, Jules, 112, 126
Lamarck, Jean Baptiste, 62
Lane, John, 118-119
"Langueur" (Verlaine), 39
Laplace, Marquis, 8
The Last Generation (Flecker), 111
"The Later Huysmans" (Symons), 112
Le Latin mystique (Gourmont), 89
Lautréamont, Comte de, 33, 36, 96
Lazare (Barbier), 21
Le Fanu, J. Sheridan, 121
Le Gallienne, Richard, 109
Lee, Vernon, 110, 121
Lee-Hamilton, Eugene, 110
Lépilliers (Lorrain), 72
Lesbia (Mendès), 127
lesbianism, 20, 72-73, 127
"Lesbos" (Baudelaire), 16
"Le Léthé" (Baudelaire), 16
Lettres à l'Amazone (Gourmont), 89
Lettres à Sixtine (Gourmont), 85
Lettres de ma chaumière (Mirbeau), 100
Lettres d'un satyre (Gourmont), 89
Lévi, Eliphas, 51
Lilith (Gourmont), 89
"Les Litanies de Satan" (Baudelaire), 13, 17, 111
literary Satanism, 12-13, 17, 35, 45, 50-51, 70, 85, 97
Le Livre de Monelle (Schwob), 127
Le Livre des masques (Gourmont), 88, 95-96

Lombard, Jean, 34
Lombroso, Cesare, 62-63, 111
The Lord of the Dark Red Star (Eugene Lee-Hamilton), 110
Lorrain, Jean, 20, 37, 42, 58, 60, 68-85, 88, 97-98, 100, 107, 111, 120, 124-125, 127
Loti, Pierre, 72, 104, 129
Louis XIV, French King, 10
Louÿs, Pierre, 20, 34, 75, 127, 129
Lovecraft, H. P., 132
Loveman, Samuel, 132
Lucian, 127
Lucius Apuleius, 45
Luscignole (Mendès), 127
Luyken, Jan, 48
Lyrical Ballads (Wordsworth & Coleridge), 12
Ma religion (Tolstoy), 99
Machen, Arthur, 119-121
Madame Bovary (Flaubert), 34
"Madame Salamandre" (Lorrain), 71
Mademoiselle de Maupin (Gautier), 20, 73
Maeterlinck, Maurice, 109, 128
La Maison de la vielle (Mendès), 127
La Maison Philibert (Lorrain), 76
Maizeroy, René, 72
Mallarmé, Stéphane, 18, 32, 35-37, 42, 45, 65, 86, 89-90, 112, 118, 125
Marius the Epicurean (Pater), 110
Mark Antony, Roman statesman, 20
Markham, Edwin, 131
La Marquise de Sade (Rachilde), 57, 129
Marthe, histoire d'une fille (Huysmans), 42
"The Masque of the Red Death" (Poe), 23
Maupassant, Guy de, 71-72, 100, 108
Mauritius, 17
Melomaniacs (Huneker), 130
Memoirs of a Woman of Pleasure (Cleland), 106
Mendès, Catulle, 37, 69, 71, 74, 86, 126-127
Mendès, Judith—SEE: Gautier, Judith

Méphistophéla (Mendès), 127
Mercier, Louis-Sébastien, 8
Mercure de France (newspaper), 71, 86, 89
Merlette (Gourmont), 85
Merrill, Stuart, 130
"Les Métamorphoses du vampire" (Baudelaire), 16
Michel, Georges—SEE: Mikhaël, Ephraïm
Michelet, Jules, 50, 52, 70, 103
Mikhaël, Ephraïm, 126
Milton, John, 12-13
Mimes (Schwob), 127
Mirbeau, Octave, 58, 86, 97-107, 124-125
modernism, 134
Moll Flanders (Defoe), 106
Le Monde (magazine), 85
Monet, Claude, 100
Monsieur de Bougrelon (Lorrain), 76
Monsieur de Phocas (Lorrain), 37, 71, 76-83, 107
Monsieur Vénus (Rachilde), 57, 71, 129
Montesquieu, Baron, 6-8, 14, 39, 90, 108
Montesquiou, Robert, Comte de, 42, 70-72
Montmartre, France, 69-70, 73
Moralités légendaries (Laforgue), 126
More, Thomas, 102
Moréas, Jean, 70
Moreau, Gustave, 36-37, 44-45, 48, 70, 79
Moreau, Jeanne, 106
Moreau de Tours, Joseph, 59, 62-63, 111
Moro, Antonio, 80
"La Morte amoureuse" (Gautier), 19
La Morte de Tintagiles (Maeterlinck), 128
Mr. Incoul's Misadventure (Saltus), 130
"The Murders in the Rue Morgue" (Poe), 22-23
My First Two Thousand Years (Viereck & Eldridge), 131
Napoléon I, French Emperor, 10, 99
Narcissus, 80

"Narkiss" (Lorrain), 80
Narrative of Arthur Gordon Pym of Nantucket (Poe), 44
National Observer (magazine), 122
The Natural Philosophy of Love (Gourmont)—SEE: *Physique de l'amour*
naturalism, 31, 42, 50, 63, 100
nature, 10, 13, 27-28, 33, 44, 115, 117, 124, 135, 137
neo-Gothic architecture, 11
Nero, Roman Emperor, 7
Nerval, Gérard de, 17, 33-34, 36, 104
The New Medusa (Eugene Lee-Hamilton), 110
Newton, Isaac, Sir, 8
Nietzsche, Friedrich, 89, 93, 95, 111, 120
A Night in the Luxembourg (Gourmont)—SEE: *Une Nuit au Luxembourg*
Nobel Prize for Literature, 99
noble savage, 8
Nono (Rachilde), 129
Nordau, Max, 65, 91
Normandy, France, 68-69, 79, 98, 100
La Nouvelle Héloïse (Rousseau), 9
La Nouvelle Justine (Sade), 9
Une Nuit au Luxembourg (Gourmont), 88-89, 94
"Une Nuit de Cléopâtre" (Gautier), 20
L'Oblat (Huysmans), 52
Odysseus, 36
Oeuvres complètes (Baudelaire), 23
L'Oiseau bleu (Maeterlinck), 128
"Omphale" (Gautier), 19
"The Opium-Smoker" (Symons), 110
Order of the Golden Dawn, 121
L'Ordre (newspaper), 98
orientalism, 11-12, 17, 34, 102, 104, 110, 129
Oxford University, 119, 122
Paget, Violet—SEE: Lee, Vernon
Pall Mall Gazette (magazine), 73
"Pall-Malls" (Lorrain column), 73, 80
Pamela; or, Virtue Rewarded (Richardson), 106

Paracelsus, 55
"Les Paradis artificiels" (Baude-
laire), 17
Paradise Lost (Milton), 12-13
Paris, France, 8, 10, 15, 19-21,
23, 27, 42, 47, 50-52, 57, 66,
68, 71, 74-77, 79-80, 84-85,
98, 108, 117, 124, 127, 130-
131, 133
Le Parnasse contemporain (Men-
dès, ed.), 35, 37-38
Parnassian poets, 21, 26, 35, 37
Paroles d'un révolté (Kropotkin),
99
Pastels in Prose (Merrill), 130
Pater, Walter, 109-110
Patrice (Gourmont), 85
"Péhor" (Gourmont), 87, 92
Péladin, Joséphin, 51, 97, 121-
122, 128
"Le Pèlerin du silence" (Gour-
mont), 89
Le Pèlerin du silence (Gourmont),
89
"Les Pelléastres" (Lorrain), 76
Penelope, 36
Petits Poèmes en prose (Baude-
laire), 23
Petronius, 45
A Phantom Lover (Lee), 121
La Philosophie dans le boudoir
(Sade), 9
Phocas, Byzantine Emperor, 82
Phocas, Saint, 82
Phocas le gardinier (Viélé-Grif-
fin), 82
*Physique de l'amour, essai sur
l'instinct sexuel* (Gourmont),
89, 93-94
The Picture of Dorian Gray
(Wilde), 42, 46, 112-115
"Le Pied de momie" (Gautier), 19
Plato and Platonism, 11, 35, 91
Les Pleisirs et les jours (Proust),
75
Poe, Edgar Allan, 16, 19, 22-23,
36, 44, 54, 65, 69, 73, 127,
130-132
Poèmes saturniens (Verlaine), 40
Poésies (Comte de Lautréamont as
Isidore Ducasse), 33
Poésies (Mallarmé), 35-36
Les Poètes maudits (Verlaine), 35,
39-41, 64

*Pope Jacynthe and Other Fantas-
tic Tales* (Lee), 121
Pougy, Liane de, 74
Pound, Ezra, 89, 94
Pozzi, Doctor, 74, 76
Pre-Raphaelites, 65, 110
La Première maîtresse (Mendès),
127
"Les Prétendants" (Moreau :
painting), 36-37, 79
"Prince Alberic and the Snake
Lady" (Lee), 121
Prince Zaleski (Shiel), 119
La Princesse des ténèbres (Rach-
ilde), 129
La Princesse Maleine (Maeter-
linck), 128
La Princesse sous verre (Lorrain),
76
Princesses d'ivoire et d'ivresse
(Lorrain), 68
Prometheus Unbound (Shelley),
13
"Prose pours Des Esseintes" (Mal-
larmé), 35
Proses moroses (Gourmont), 89-
90
Proust, Marcel, 73, 75
Le Puits de Sainte Clare (France),
45
The Purple Cloud (Shiel), 120
Quarterly Review (magazine), 108
Queensberry, Marquis of, 122
Rabelais, François, 128
Rachilde, 42, 57, 71, 75, 77, 85-
86, 89, 128-129
Rais, Gilles de, 50-52
Ransome, Arthur, 88
"Realism and Decadence in
French Literature" (Barry),
108
Redon, Odilon, 37
Régnier, Henri de, 75
Renoir, Jean, 106
"Rêve d'enfer" (Flaubert), 35
La Révolte des anges (France), 45,
98-99, 107
Le Revue des deux mondes
(magazine), 16
Revue fantaisiste (magazine), 37
Rhymers' Club, 109-110
Ribot, Théodule, 27, 64
Richardson, Samuel, 106
Richepin, Jean, 70

Rimbaud, Arthur, 38-39, 77, 82, 110, 124-125
"La Robe blanche" (Gourmont), 87
Robespierre, Maximilien, 9
robinsonades, 43
Rodenbach, Georges, 75, 126-128
Rodin, Auguste, 100
Le Roi au masque d'or (Schwob), 127
Rolfe, Fr.—SEE: Corvo, Baron
Roman Empire, 6-7, 15, 27, 45, 54, 128
romanticism, 11-13, 19, 21, 23, 26-27, 37, 89, 102, 110, 120, 126, 129
Rops, Félicien, 37
Rosicrucians, 51, 122
Rossetti, Christina, 121
Rossetti, Dante Gabriel, 110
Rostand, Edmond, 72
"Rougon-Macquart" series (Zola), 63
Rousseau, Jean-Jacques, 8-11, 13, 26-27, 33, 124
Sabatier, Apollonie, Madame, 17
Sade, Marquis de, 9-10, 13, 27, 33, 45, 102-103, 106
sadism, 102
Sagesse (Verlaine), 39-40
Sainte-Beuve, Charles-Augustin, 18, 21-22, 25, 63
Une Saison en enfer (Rimbaud), 39, 82
Salammbô (Flaubert), 34
Salomé (Wilde), 119, 127
Saltus, Edgar, 130
Sand, George, 89
Le Sang des dieux (Lorrain), 70
La Satanisme et magie (Bois), 51
The Savoy (magazine), 119
Schlegel, August, 12
Schopenhauer, Arthur, 27, 89, 93, 95
Schwob, Marcel, 80, 127
Sébastien Roch (Mirbeau), 101
Sedan, Battle of (1870), 10
Sensations et souvenirs (Lorrain), 73
sensibilité (literary movement), 11-12
sex in literature, 87, 91-93
"Shadow—A Parable" (Poe), 23
Shapes in the Fire (Shiel), 119-120

Shelley, Percy Bysshe, 12-13
Shiel, M. P., 119-120
"Silence—A Fable" (Poe), 23
Silhouettes (Symons), 110
The Sins of the Fathers: Decadence in France, 1870-1914 (Birkett), 112
Sirens (Greek mythological characters), 70
Sixtine (Gourmont), 85
"Smarh" (Flaubert), 35
Smith, Clark Ashton, 132
"Solitude: Anywhere Out of the World" (Ephraïm Mikhaël), 126
Somerset, Arthur, Lord, 69
Le Songe d'une femme (Gourmont), 89
Sonnets of the Wingless Hours (Eugene Lee-Hamilton), 110
Sonyeuse (Lorrain), 69
Sorbonne (France), 8
La Sorcière (Michelet), 50
Spirite (Gautier), 20
spleen, 21, 30, 64
"Spleen" (Baudelaire), 26, 30, 39-40
Le Spleen de Paris (Baudelaire), 23
Stanislavsky, Konstantin, 64
Starrett, Vincent, 132
Stead, W. T., 73-74
Stenbock, Eric, Count, 119-120
"Stéphane Mallarmé and the Idea of Decadence" (Gourmont), 90
Sterling, George, 131-132
Stevenson, Robert Louis, 127
Stoker, Bram, 121
The Stone Dragon and Other Tragic Romances (Gilchrist), 119
Stories Toto Told Me (Corvo), 119
"Stratagems" (Gourmont), 87
Studies of Death: Romantic Tales (Stenbock), 119-120
Sue, Eugène, 33
surrealism, 31, 134
Swinburne, Algernon Charles, 69, 108, 110
symbolism, 31, 35, 70, 86-87, 89, 100, 109, 112, 124-125, 128
The Symbolist Movement in Literature (Symons), 112

151

Symons, Arthur, 40, 109-110, 112, 119-120, 124
syphilis, 55-58, 74
Taine, Hippolyte, 64
Tales of Soldiers and Civilians (Bierce), 130
Tales of the Grotesque and Arabesque (Poe), 22
La Tentation de Saint Antoine (Flaubert), 34-35, 37, 70
"Les Tentations, ou Éros, Plutus, et la Gloire" (Baudelaire), 25
Thaïs (France), 34
The Three Brides (Toorop : painting), 78
Tinan, Jean de, 75
Tolstoy, Leo, 65, 99
Toorop, Jan, 78
Toulouse-Lautrec, Henri de, 69
"La Tragédie humaine" (France), 98
Très Russe (Lorrain), 72
Le Tréteau (Lorrain), 72
Trevières, France, 98
Trinity College (Dublin), 121-122
Trois contes (Flaubert), 35
tuberculosis, 55, 57-58, 69, 76, 88
Turgot, Anne-Robert, 8-9
The Twilight of the Gods (Garnett), 121
Under the Hill (Beardsley), 119
universal history, 8
Utopia (More), 102
Vallette, Alfred, 71, 86
Vathek (Beckford), 11-12
The Velvet Path (Gourmont)— SEE: *Le Chemin de velours*
Verlaine, Paul, 18, 20, 32, 35-36, 38-41, 45, 64-65, 72, 75, 77, 109, 125-126
"La Verre du sang" (Lorrain), 58
Le Vice errant (Lorrain), 76

Victorian era, 108, 120-122
La Vie parisienne (magazine), 76, 85
Viélé-Griffin, Francis, 82
Viereck, George Sylvester, 131
Vies imaginaires (Schwob), 127
Villiers de L'Isle-Adam, 42, 86, 94, 96, 100, 126, 128
Les Vingt-et-un jours d'un neurasthénique (Mirbeau), 106
Virgil, 45
"The Virgin of the Seven Daggers" (Lee), 121
Visionaries (Huneker), 130
Voltaire, 99, 102
Volupté (Sainte-Beuve), 18, 21
Voyage en Orient (Nerval), 34
Wagner, Richard, 36, 44-45, 65
Walpole, Horace, 11
Waterloo, Battle of (1815), 10
Watts-Dunton, Theodore, 110
Weird Tales (magazine), 132
The Were-Wolf (C. Housman), 119
What Is Art? (Tolstoy), 65
Wilde, Cyril, 115
Wilde, Oscar, 42-43, 46, 69, 80, 108-123, 127, 133-134
Wilde, Vyvyan, 115
Willy, 129
"A Wine of Wizardry" (Sterling), 131-132
Wordsworth, William, 12
World War I, 124
Yeats, William Butler, 109, 121
Yellow Book (magazine), 118-119, 121
L'Ymagier (magazine), 86
Zo'har (Mendès), 127
Zola, Émile, 42, 50, 63, 71, 74, 99-100, 108
Zutistes (French literary group), 70